Elements in the Renaissance
edited by
John Henderson
*Birkbeck, University of London, and Wolfson College,
University of Cambridge*
Jonathan K. Nelson
Syracuse University Florence

THE FABRIC OF WAR

*The Material Culture and Social
Lives of Banners in Renaissance
Europe*

John Gagné
University of Sydney

Timothy McCall
Villanova University

Shaftesbury Road, Cambridge CB2 8EA, United Kingdom

One Liberty Plaza, 20th Floor, New York, NY 10006, USA

477 Williamstown Road, Port Melbourne, VIC 3207, Australia

314–321, 3rd Floor, Plot 3, Splendor Forum, Jasola District Centre, New Delhi – 110025, India

103 Penang Road, #05–06/07, Visioncrest Commercial, Singapore 238467

Cambridge University Press is part of Cambridge University Press & Assessment, a department of the University of Cambridge.

We share the University's mission to contribute to society through the pursuit of education, learning and research at the highest international levels of excellence.

www.cambridge.org
Information on this title: www.cambridge.org/9781009571807

DOI: 10.1017/9781009364256

© John Gagné and Timothy McCall 2025

This publication is in copyright. Subject to statutory exception and to the provisions of relevant collective licensing agreements, no reproduction of any part may take place without the written permission of Cambridge University Press & Assessment.

When citing this work, please include a reference to the DOI 10.1017/9781009364256

First published 2025

A catalogue record for this publication is available from the British Library

ISBN 978-1-009-57180-7 Hardback
ISBN 978-1-009-36422-5 Paperback
ISSN 2631-9101 (online)
ISSN 2631-9098 (print)

Cambridge University Press & Assessment has no responsibility for the persistence or accuracy of URLs for external or third-party internet websites referred to in this publication and does not guarantee that any content on such websites is, or will remain, accurate or appropriate.

For EU product safety concerns, contact us at Calle de José Abascal, 56, 1°, 28003 Madrid, Spain, or email eugpsr@cambridge.org

The Fabric of War

The Material Culture and Social Lives of Banners in Renaissance Europe

Elements in the Renaissance

DOI: 10.1017/9781009364256
First published online: July 2025

John Gagné
University of Sydney

Timothy McCall
Villanova University

Author for correspondence: John Gagné, john.gagne@sydney.edu.au

Abstract: This Element traces the rich history of flags and banners in Renaissance Europe through a critical analysis of the cultural, ideological, material, and artistic histories of these complex and ubiquitous objects. It examines banners as numinous textiles that animated and adorned battle, energized and embellished armies, constructed and celebrated victory. Though flags are often investigated as mere symbols to be deciphered – as heraldic code revealing identity – they were vibrant and charismatic textiles whose mutability, movement, and multivalency constituted their appeal and salience. Banners propelled their viewers not only to decipher or identify but also to act.

Keywords: flags, war, material culture, Renaissance, Art History

© John Gagné and Timothy McCall 2025

ISBNs: 9781009571807 (HB), 9781009364225 (PB), 9781009364256 (OC)
ISSNs: 2631-9101 (online), 2631-9098 (print)

Contents

	Introduction	1
1	Fire	7
2	Blood	12
3	Makers	31
4	Anghiari	42
5	Gifts	55
6	Water	66
	References	93

Introduction

Leonardo da Vinci's *Battle of Anghiari* intended for Florence's town hall would have been a brutal, vicious painting: an exceedingly terrible painting, in the Italian Renaissance understanding of *terribile*, inducing terror, dread, and awe. Since Leonardo never completed the fresco, we can only know his conception from studies and copies (Figure 1). Milanese and Florentine warriors clash, pulled into this tumultuous vortex. Humans and horses collide and cry out. Soldiers are mercilessly trampled underfoot. Swords and spears are vigorously raised and thrusted. There is little doubt that bodies will be maimed. At the very center of this classic Leonardesque knot of men and horses, hands grasp a flag-bearer's staff toward which a fearsome blade or two plunge down, set to separate these gripping hands from their bodies. The most dramatic of the sword-wielding, shrieking men has the sharp tip of a broken flagpole (in some copies a lance) pointed right in his face. The action and tension, in all its brutality, revolves around the fight for the battle standard. This is a savage combat-to-the-death over a piece of cloth. These men are clearly ready to die for the flag they struggle to guard or capture. And indeed, when the Florentines seized Milanese banners at Anghiari in 1440, victory was assured; in the words of one of Florence's war commissioners present at the battle, "our captain charged . . . to assault the enemy's standard, and having taken it, they were routed."[1] But why is it, then, that this key to the painting, with few exceptions, is so rarely thematized by Renaissance art historians?[2] This blindspot calls us to look anew at Leonardo's ambitious, if never realized, masterpiece of Renaissance painting – a prestigious commission intended for Florence's politically charged council chamber and soon to be forever paired with another near-mythic fresco, by no less an artist than Michelangelo. In Leonardo's famed *Battle of Anghiari*, we must recognize an image, at its core, about a flag.

This Element traces the rich history of banners and flags in Renaissance Europe as dynamic, vibrant, and charismatic objects and interprets their function and meaning. We excavate, from multiple perspectives, the work banners performed in cultures, particularly in arenas of war. We seek to understand the agency and efficacy that they possessed or were imputed. Banners were tools of power that animated and not only adorned battle, energized and not only embellished armies, created and not only celebrated victory. Not merely the fixed ground of symbols or static heraldic code, these were vibrant textiles whose mutability, movement, and multivalency constituted their appeal and salience. Banners and flags might typically be thought of as emblems of identity, decorated with ossified imagery, yet we argue that they were spirited and active, both materially and in broader social and political terms. Though they may seem

---

[1] Capponi, 1731: Column 1194–5. [2] Fehrenbach, 2007.

Figure 1 Peter Paul Rubens, over the drawing of a sixteenth-century artist after Leonardo da Vinci's *Fight for the Standard*, ca. 1550s and 1600. Black chalk, pen, brown ink, brown wash, and oil. Paris, Musée du Louvre, Département des Arts Graphiques, 20.271. Alamy Photo.

insubstantial when imagined and represented flitting in the wind, Renaissance flags were undeniably weighty things.

Like magnets, banners drew the eyes and bodies of men and women toward them. And they still do. We investigate the vexed historiography of flags, and we insist that contemporary mobilizations of banners demanding a return to past traditions and abhorrent values require further analysis. It is not enough to explain recent (Neo-Nazi) Neo-Medieval imagery adorning flags in twenty-first-century white supremacist rallies as only misused signs and symbols. Missing from recent interpretations of flags as stationary bearers of symbols – as with most accounts of early modern flags more generally – is a reckoning with the fact that they are lively textile media that carve out and aggressively claim space.

Though some categories of Renaissance banners are familiar to art historians, chiefly Italian confraternal *gonfaloni*, the flags and standards mustered in war and civic conflict have been, by and large, ignored even by Renaissance scholarship's recent vigorous material and textile turns.[3] We appreciate banners and flags in motion, mobile and portable, borne by people and energized by the

---

[3] Rihouet, 2019; Richardson, 2024.

air in which they fluttered and curled. Crucial to our investigation is close attention to banners' materiality: not just their textiles, often iridescent silks, but also the radiant adornment that embellished them, such as gold leaf, precious metals, shimmering fringe, and loads of pearls. These scintillating objects were activated both by their flickering movement and by the visual effects of silk and gold. They were dangerous and daunting (and, with their staffs, used as weapons); they were beautiful and brilliant (made of the most sumptuous dyes, metals, and textiles available); and they were awe-inspiring and intimidating (promising triumph and glory, bloodshed and peril). Rippling in the air, they projected authority; planted in the ground, they claimed entire continents. Vexillologists stress that flags should be designed for maximum clarity and legibility. Their imagery may seem almost fossilized, yet flags' inevitable motion and animation confirm, as Richard Trexler asserted, that they are "the least fixed of representations."[4]

This Element explores banners' sensory and phenomenological effects. We imagine them in concert within Renaissance soundscapes – trumpets and drums resounding, bodies marching, voices chanting and singing, and fabric whipping in the wind. We consider too their life cycles – the social biographies of textiles that experienced ritualized births and deaths. Ceremonial blessings enlivened flags, turning them into sacralized relics whose potency was clear both when paraded on the battlefield and when integrated into dynastic or ecclesiastical treasuries. Renaissance banners, moreover, served eloquently within gift economies and to produce and maintain networks of aristocratic and civic alliance. Though their social lives and histories might inhere for generations when hanging in castle or cathedral rafters, this enshrinement also deadened them. So too did their entrance into museum collections, which constituted a sort of resecularization. Displayed flat and motionless, the dynamic textiles and surfaces are disempowered, not merely decontextualized as are all Renaissance objects housed in museums but devoid of the vibrancy and animation furnished by their shimmering surfaces and rippling movement, the life emptied out of them.

In an important study of the modern flag of India, Arundhati Virmani reveals the work that flags do to forge but also fracture identities, to amplify nationalism, and to fashion both political belonging and exclusion.[5] Flags stand in for identity, to be sure. Much like the colors and devices of heraldry, to which they are related, flags were always socially embedded. Manifesting both personal and corporate affiliation, they sorted and classed people and made bodies legible. As something like the exuviae of military valor, flags – once captured – promised the possession

---

[4] Trexler, 1984: 359.   [5] Virmani, 2008.

of enemies' honor in material form. Banners were not just markers but makers of personhood, existing and operating between presence and representation. Crucially, we insist that meanings enacted by these textiles are hardly exhausted by the symbolic.

These fabric semaphores were never stable in meaning. Mobile and immediate, auratic and vital, banners were also unruly and uncontrollable. They identified, but also deceived; arranged, but also misdirected; commemorated, but also misremembered. They propelled viewers not only to interpret and identify but also to act. These textiles took a wide array of forms and formats, moreover, and were not consistently categorized by the sources that describe them. We aim to account for flags in their material and visual complexity and multiplicity, rather than to classify them within set taxonomies. Thus, we do not propose a typology of Renaissance war banners, though by looking astride the Alps and by taking brief stock from around the globe, we hope to show how central this material culture was to aristocratic, civic, and military cultures of display. This Element is not comprehensive and it circumvents the pedantic vexillological distinctions that tend to limit rather than enable analysis. Instead, it introduces new models for interpreting the power, operations, and effects of banners. In writing it, we also realized that historians have all but ignored the potential for cross-cultural analyses of these objects. Although we include some comparative interpretations, this is not a global history. It seems increasingly clear to us, however, that such wide-ranging histories should be written.

The interpretive tools and frameworks provided by recent studies of material culture – the social lives of things, theories of prestation, and attention to the visual, sensory phenomena of objects on the move – equip us to understand banners as active agents and consequential objects. These were, after all, just strips of fabric. Yet people willingly died for them, and not just for the idea of them, or what they stood for, but for the objects themselves. Premodern societies sustained what we call "banner cults," in which devotees treated flags as transcendent relics. This practice is exemplified in a small leather box adorned with gleamy cameos and silver crests. It was designed to contain not just holy artifacts but also the pennant of French King François I, seized along with the monarch himself at the Battle of Pavia in 1525 (Figure 2). The military trophy and religious tokens within it acted as mutual amplifiers, linking God's providence with François' defeat. Indeed, much like sacred images, whether *Madonnas* painted by Luke or miraculously transferred faces of Christ, banners frequently had doubles and triples. They were copied and recopied in substitutional chains to save their significance from the depredations of time.[6]

---

[6] Nagel and Wood, 2010: 29–34.

Figure 2 Spanish artisans, leather box for King François I's pennant taken at the Battle of Pavia, 1525. Baltimore, The Walters Art Museum, 73.1. Photo: The Walters Art Museum.

The ineluctable disintegration of gossamer textiles did not always destroy their meaning; deterioration provided opportunities for renewal and reimagination, and for new futures and pasts to emerge. Throughout this Element, we trace these fraught tensions between banners' fragile materiality and their resilient symbolic values.

In a groundbreaking study of the 1378 Florentine Ciompi revolts, Richard Trexler underscored the agency and dynamism of flags – the work that they do – by illuminating the ways that they shaped social space, produced and reflected shifts of power, and (re)organized society. Without banners, "a society cannot defend itself against the enemy; lacking them the mind's eye cannot picture the parts or integration of collectivities." For Trexler, flags were not mere symbols; in action, they "lose the dead scholarly skin that had them only 'stand for' something else."[7] His prescient study anticipated the recent turn to the performative and phenomenological aspects of art in motion. Trexler declared incisively that "[p]hysical activity is meaning," and he showed the ways that flags "bring us close to experience." We are inspired by Trexler's insistence to "descend to the barricades to discover what that importance [of flags] was" rather than view conflict only from above or interpret banners in stasis and removed from the bodies that conveyed them.[8] Of course, associations and

---

[7] Trexler, 1984: 357. Also, Cohn, 2008: 177–204.   [8] Trexler, 1984: 358, 391.

meanings imputed to flags were as contingent as the textiles themselves. Flags promise stability and fixity but always shift in the wind.

Early modern banners organized battlefields in practical terms, identifying commanders, nobles, and rallying points, directing companies and calvaries, and communicating to friend and foe alike.[9] In his *Art of War* (*Dell'arte della guerra*), Niccolò Machiavelli commented that an army showed itself to be well trained if its battalions assumed their proper places as the captain's standard was lifted and trumpet sounded.[10] Textiles raised into the air signal the presence of bodies below. Armies, war-tents, castles, and ships all teem with human life. The undulating movement of fabric in the breeze reports on the living who hoist it: cloth breathes, as people do. This will to motion making flags energetic objects informs our interpretations and helps us see them as spirited rather than impassive.[11] Alternatively, when banners adorn ceremonial sites such as tombs or memorials, they signal the corpses below, marking lives cut off. A flag can be the ghostly apparition of a human presence.

Banners were prophylactic and protective, shielding those amassed underneath. Yet, they also drew violence to them, for in many cases their bearers (or even their maker) paid the ultimate price, as we shall see. When the banner was lost, so was the cause. In 1310, in the thick of a popular rebellion against Venetian rule in Trieste, a woman on a balcony dropped a stone on the head of the conspirators' flag-bearer passing underneath. The banner fell to the ground and its staff shattered. Straight away, the rebels scattered, essentially putting an end to the uprising. This balcony-warrior and champion of Venice was rewarded by the Council of Ten with fixed rent for life and the right to fly the flag of San Marco.[12]

Banners were tremendously charismatic. In 1521, a green Moorish banner that had been captured in the thirteenth-century Reconquista and enshrined in Seville's church of Omnium Sanctorum energized the *Motín del Pendón Verde*, a popular revolt that would long resonate in the town's history.[13] A fifteenth-century Florentine battle song urging men at arms to follow and chase their banner conveys something of the ferocity of the exhortations that troops heard on the battlefield, rippling textiles always in sight, dynamic motivators to be staunchly defended or recklessly plundered: "Who will be the bravest?/ We shall follow the standard./ Hurry up bold soldiers of the Sforza,/ of Bologna and of France./ Until they are prisoners and broken,/ forward, valiant and bold men/ good and well-trained soldiers,/ Clear away that ugly mob!"[14] In 1499, Maximilian, the King of the Romans and later Holy Roman Emperor, urged

---

[9] Groebner, 2004: 125–46; Jones, 2010: 11–37. [10] Machiavelli, 1869: 77–8.
[11] Schwering, 1974: 66. [12] Cohn, 2008: 185. [13] Knezevic, 2014.
[14] McGee, 1983: 300.

his soldiers to "follow the standard, even against one's own father, son, or brother."[15] Time and again fighters mobilized, weaponized, obeyed, seized, trembled before, and above all pursued banners. Flags were also sequestered, searched for, stockpiled, and fiercely defended precisely because of their extraordinary potential and efficacy. Banners provided legitimacy to the acts carried out below them, and they granted bearers the right to enact these deeds.

In the sections that follow, we closely examine the evocative materiality, vibrant visual effects, and skilled makers of banners. We explore stories of their ideation, production, purchase, gifting, display, and archiving to interpret their material and social lives. Banners embodied the prestige and personhood of owners and communities, enough to become trophies as valuable as victory itself. This Element concludes by setting European flags in a global context. This allows us to frame our study across diverse traditions while simultaneously tracing banners across oceans and continents as they become the archetypal object of seizure and domination in the colonial age. To begin, however, we first turn to the pre-Renaissance history of flags, and to their more recent, and doomed, historiography.

1 Fire

In 1935, Otto Huth (1906–98) – a member of Heinrich Himmler's *Ahnenerbe* thinktank and a specialist in Indo-Germanic cultures at the Reich University in Strasbourg – began a postdoctoral research project titled *Vesta*, a study of ancient fire cults published in 1943.[16] Huth belonged to a generation of Nazi scholars engaged in what they called *Sinnbildforschung*, or ideographic research: an effort to trace an Aryan cultural genealogy deep into the middle ages, antiquity, and prehistory through symbolic cultural forms. The pseudo-scholarly methods developed by Huth and his colleagues aimed in part to identify concrete images (*Bilder*) that bespoke cultural ideas (*Sinn*). Passion for these ideographs drove the study of archaic Germanic runes such as the triskelion, the fulmen, and the symbol now inextricably linked to the National Socialist flag, the swastika.[17] Such cultic associations of fire were on full display in the torch relay – a new invention, albeit framed as primeval – in the 1936 Olympic Games in Berlin.[18] Perhaps with such loaded images in fresh memory, level-headed scholars across Europe rejected the majority of Huth's findings about fire cults.[19]

---

[15] Pélissier, 1912: 14.   [16] Huth, 1943.   [17] Mees, 2008: 197–200; Junginger, 2017.
[18] Bernett, Funck, and Woggon, 1996: 15–16.
[19] Lambrechts, 1945: 412–14; Goldammer, 1956: 24.

Very little intellectual value can be salvaged from Huth's study. It does, however, draw attention to the obsession of German-speaking scholars in the 1930s and 1940s with flags, which Huth called "the image of fire."[20] A veritable flood of studies on the long histories of medieval flags rolled off presses in these years, no doubt stimulated by wartime jingoism or curiosity to clarify the histories of the banners under which modern Europeans were fighting each other. The prewar scholar who made the most valuable inroads toward comprehending early European flags as instruments of sovereignty was the Crusades historian Carl Erdmann (1898–1945). Flags abounded in the Crusader chronicles of the late middle ages, and Erdmann found them to be telling indices of papal and imperial strategies of domination. But his politics were a long way from Otto Huth's. The years Erdmann devoted to studying the zealous and violent pursuit of medieval empire predisposed him to distrust the Nazi regime, whose agents eventually blocked his career and drafted him into military service. Erdmann died as an interpreter in a Croatian camp only weeks before the end of the war.[21] He appreciated that flags could be understood not just for their primordial cultic force but, perhaps as a consequence of it, also for their mobilization as seductive tools of political authority.

Thus, by 1945, the most probing European scholar of flags had lost his life, while Nazi heraldry and its pseudo-scholarly histories had also toxified the study of flags, steering Germanophone scholars away from the topic for generations – until very recently.[22] The mid-century bibliography we still employ to investigate the history of European flags is enmeshed with this legacy: one in which arguments about medieval symbolic power disguised darker disputes about modern political fortunes. "Do medieval banners and modern flags frighten historians?" asked Michel Pastoureau, the French historian of heraldry, in 2004. They do, he suggested, precisely because of this recent history of "distorted uses, excessive passion, and ideological spirals."[23] Flags have become objects difficult to disentangle from politics past and present. Yet, now more than ever it seems essential to do so, as flags have dramatically energized white supremacist and radical right protests and riots in recent years in the United States and beyond, including Neo-Confederate troupes of "flaggers" and Trumpist flotillas or "boat parades." Hundreds of banners borne by men and women storming the US Capitol contributed to the turbulent attack of the January 6 insurrection in 2021. This sea of flags united insurgents under a shared banner, as varied as the many flags were (Figure 3). Their swirling, terrible animation mobilized the insurrectionists below. Flagstaffs, moreover,

---

[20] Huth, 1943: 154–7.   [21] Fink, 1947: 355–7; Cantor, 1991: 403–4.
[22] Weber, 2006: 531–3; Weber, 2011: 10.
[23] Pastoureau, 2004: 275–6. Also, Virmani, 2008: 4–5.

Figure 3 January 6, 2021, insurrection. Photo Michael Nigro, Pacific Press Media/Alamy Photo.

were wielded as weapons – one man was convicted and another charged with assault with flagpoles. The horrific scene took our minds to the fifteenth century, evoking something of the clamor and violence of the Renaissance battlefield. This, in a strange way, is the living legacy of the cynical *Sinnbildforschung* of Otto Huth and others. For those Nazi researchers, collapsing the present into the past was part of the appeal. Flags were the perfect ideographs: They functioned as material instantiations of deeply rooted cultural concepts. Their multivalency made them ideal ideological tools across centuries. In fact, banner worship around the world remains haunted by the specters of jingoism up to our own time. Flags were, and continue to be, nodes of passion: images of fire in more than one sense.

Otto Huth's *Vesta* inspired researchers to reject its racist suppositions about ancient fire cults, but he was not wrong at least about the strong association between flame and flag: The semantic and symbolic link between flickering fire and billowing cloth can be traced into deep histories. Vegetius, whose late-antique treatise on military science circulated everywhere in medieval Europe, explained the varieties of signals that armies could employ in battle. Aural signs included human shouts and words (*vocalia*) along with horns, bugles, and other instruments (*semivocalia*). Visual signs (*muta*) included things raised into the air, such as "eagles, dragons, insignia, pennants (*flammulae*), crests, plumes," along with other semaphores like dust, fire, smoke, and wooden beams.[24]

---

[24] Formisano, 2003: 206 (Vegetius, *Epitoma rei militaris*, III.5).

Eagles and dragons referred to the major totemic standards of the Roman army: The eagle represented the entire legion, while the dragon stood for the smaller cohort.[25] Dragon flags (*draco*, pl. *dracones*), which the Romans seem to have imported from the Near East, themselves conjured an image of fire. Held aloft on poles, tubes of crimson silk billowed in the wake of gruesome metallic dragon or wolf heads, effectively conjuring snaky, fulminous bodies. Ancient sources describe not just movement but also a hissing noise as wind passed through the metal head.[26] *Dracones* lasted for centuries in post-Roman Europe: a horseman carries one aloft in a Carolingian psalter (Figure 4), with sparks appearing to shoot from its mouth. In 1246, English King Henry III had a *draco* made of red silk and gold, reputedly fitted with a movable tongue and sparkling gemstone eyes.[27] This multimedia flag – richly adorned, fiercely life-like, and perhaps even literally flame-throwing – harnessed the restless fury of mythical creatures to conjure fear. Even when metal dragon heads and silk tubes fell out of use in the thirteenth century, the dragon transformed into an image of itself, emblazoned on heraldic paraphernalia across Europe. Appearing here too was the dragon's nemesis, the knightly Saint George, a model of courtly masculinity for lords, including the dukes of Burgundy and Milan on whose banner he dramatically slayed this mythical beast.

The Romans and their inheritors even more explicitly connected flag and fire by naming, as Vegetius did, their small red military pennants *flammulae* (little flames). This emphasis on the banners' flame-like flickers reminds us that they are, ideally, in motion, energetically fluttering. They move because they are processed by their bearers below but also because wind whips them into action and enlivens their materials and forms. The name *flammula* continued in regular use in Byzantium. The Eastern Empire employed the word as its most common noun for military flags from the eleventh to the fifteenth centuries.[28] The association with fire also survived in the name of France's renowned battle standard, the Oriflamme, thus signaling its exalted status as a golden (*aurum*) flame (*flamma*). Preserved in the treasury of Saint-Denis, the Oriflamme emerged from its quiet precinct during times of need, when France's kings raised it to protect and guide them in pilgrimage, crusade, or war. In the 1370s – when the kings flew the Oriflamme regularly in their conflicts with the English – the Carmelite theologian Jean Golein linked the banner's origin to a divine vision experienced by a Byzantine emperor. The sovereign supposedly awoke to see "a horseman on a large warhorse, fully armed, holding a lance that

---

[25] Formisano, 2003: 152 (Vegetius, *Epitoma rei militaris*, II.13).   [26] Coulston, 1991: 104–14.
[27] Schramm, 1954–56: 663. Also, Jones, 2010: 43–4.   [28] Babuin, 2001: 21.

Figure 4 Psalm 59 (60), Horseman with draco, in Golden Psalter (Psalterium aureum), late ninth century. St. Gallen, Stiftsbibliothek, Cod. Sang. 22, fol. 140. Photo courtesy St. Gallen, Stiftsbibliothek.

shimmered like gold and shone like the sun. From it issued a flaming torch in the form of a blazing banner," burning so brightly that its image streaked in the emperor's eyes even after the vision had vanished.[29] With this confected story (the horseman was Charlemagne), Golein bound the Oriflamme to an imperial past, invoking Carolingian glory and even deeper histories of the first Christian Emperor Constantine's famous angelic vision promising victory under the sign of the cross.

---

[29] Durand, 1374: fol. 52r.

Despite efforts like Golein's to anchor the French standard in a recognized tradition, basic confusions about name, provenance, color, size, and design vex its long history.[30] "Oriflamme" as a proper name does not appear in sources before 1124. Moreover, vastly conflicting descriptions over the centuries invalidate the idea that the French monarchy nurtured one self-same flag through the ages. It is probable that multiple Oriflammes existed at the same time, even if the rhetoric insisted on its singularity.[31] (Any and all of them disappeared during the Revolution.) Even the most iconic European flags had doubles and triples. The mesmerizing power of fire could catch and spread easily.

2 Blood

The vivacious and life-capturing qualities of textiles infuse the Christian tradition. Medieval Europe abounded with relics of Christ's life, an incarnation in which unbounded divinity clothed itself in the mundanity of human corporeality. Fabric was integral to this tradition, because it often touched living skin and drank warm blood: cloth testifies to contact with flesh. Consider the scrap of fabric in Bruges reputedly soaked with Christ's blood, which came from Byzantium to Flanders after Constantinople's sack in 1204.[32] Think also of the seamless robe of Trier, or the miraculous Mandylion and Sudarium (Veronica's Veil), or the shroud of Turin, which may have served as a military standard and was captured in battle by a bearer of the Oriflamme.[33] With each relic, textile confirmed Christ's humanity and acted as an interface with his divinity. Christ's presence could also be carried into war in the form of a sign or banner, as Constantine did. He borrowed the Roman Empire's *vexillum* and marked it with the Christogram to make the first Christian standard (the *labarum*), or what Kurt Goldammer called both a "tutelary fetish" and "battle fetish" object.[34] The binding together of two numinous objects (staff and cloth, as in the Oriflamme vision) potently signified protective agency. Eusebius of Caesarea described the *labarum* as a sumptuous cloth hanging from a short transverse beam atop a tall, gilded spear, which now had the incidental advantage of recalling the crucifix (staffs holding up a horizontal bar would later support ecclesiastical *gonfaloni*, similarly evoking a cross for some audiences).[35] European Christian warriors regularly carried crosses and

---

[30] Loomis, 1954: 67–82; Contamine, 1973.
[31] Contamine, 1973: 218–21, 229; Six, 1905: 22n7.
[32] Huyghebaert, 1963: 174, 185.
[33] Hahn, 2017: 203–5.   [34] Goldammer, 1956: 24, 35.   [35] Fehrenbach, 2007: 403.

flag-icons into battle, consolidating in a single object "a request for protection, help, and victory."[36]

Several centuries earlier, Christ himself had come to embody the Constantinian concept of a militant, and thus standard-bearing church. Depictions of the Lamb of God possessing the *labarum* go back to late antiquity, and from the early fourteenth century artists depicted Christ carrying a banner after his resurrection. North of the Alps, the resurrected deity bears a four-tailed red *labarum* in a Rhenish homiliary now at the Walters Art Museum (Figure 5), and to the south, in Giotto's *Noli Me Tangere* in the Scrovegni Chapel, Christ's flag – white with a red cross and three tails – is explicitly a banner of victory, the cross quartered with the motto VICTOR MORTIS (Figure 6).[37] It would not be surprising if artists borrowed the concept of the Resurrection banner, marking Christ's triumph over death, from the flags of war-wagons (*carrocci*) that Italian free cities used in their battles through the thirteenth century, or perhaps from the twelfth-century Crusades. The red cross on white ground fluttered ubiquitously across late medieval Europe, often associated with specific saints such as Ambrose or George, and particularly with Christ's blood.[38] The Milanese already considered it their own flag in the 1150s, representing liberation from the threat of overlordship, as the *comune* explicitly relayed in a letter to Tortona accompanying gifts of a flag, a seal, and a trumpet.[39] In the resurrected Christ's grasp, no banner better substantiated the mystery of overcoming death, anchored as it was in real civic experiences of battling impossible odds in deadly conflicts with the emperors.

The notion that banners bespoke a form of communion between a group of people had profound implications for Europeans. Sacramentality inhered in the banners of the Swiss Cantons, for example, because they acted as tokens of individual sacrifice for the community. Swiss conflicts largely involved warring contingents of foot soldiers, and as a result the flag bound together the men who marched beneath it into a kind of corporate unity, whose shared fate and spilled blood the heraldry might even narrate. Chroniclers tell how in 1191, Berthold V, duke of Zähringen, ordered a city to be founded on the site where he caught his first major quarry, a fierce black bear, and to name the city for it (Bern). This foundation inspired the duke to bestow upon the town a shield of a black bear on a white ground.[40] That flag flew over Bern for nearly a century, until taxation disputes with the Habsburgs led to armed conflict at the Battle of Schosshalde in

---

[36] Schreiner, 2011: 29.
[37] For slightly later resurrection banners: Cassee, Berserik, and Hoyle, 1984.
[38] Erdmann, 1933–34: 38; Zug Tucci, 1985: 18–22.   [39] Erdmann, 1933–34: 41.
[40] Justinger, 1871: 8.

Figure 5 German artist, The Resurrection, with Augustinian nuns, in Homiliary, ca. 1320. Baltimore, The Walters Art Museum, W.148, fol. 2 v. Photo: The Walters Art Museum.

1289. In the tumult, Austrian opponents grabbed the bottom corner of Bern's flag, and it was only saved when the banner-bearer, Hans von Gryers (i.e., from Gruyères), sliced the cloth to release what the enemy had seized. In the ensuing defeat of Bern, the legend goes, Bernese blood saturated the white cloth, staining the banner crimson. From that moment forward, Bern's flag would display both the sword-cuts and the bloodstains of the city's dead. Illustrated chronicles depict the moment in which Gryers cuts the flag to free it from Austrian hands, an allegory of sacrificing part to save the whole (Figure 7).

Figure 6 Giotto, Noli Me Tangere, 1303–05. Padua, Scrovegni Chapel. Photo: Manuel Cohen/Art Resource, NY.

Crimson banners suggested blood for some audiences, an effect produced through expensive dyes of kermes and, later, cochineal. In towns throughout Italy, sumptuary laws reserved crimson clothing for noble classes and denied it to laboring ones. The Spanish painter and art theorist Francisco Pacheco – Diego Velázquez's teacher – reported producing enormous royal naval standards, some flown to the Americas, from crimson-dyed silk "enriched" with gold, silver, and colors in oil.[41] The lavishness of crimson silks (adorned or not) was readily apparent, common knowledge for Renaissance viewers; red banners' color and materiality produced meaning that surpassed that of mere symbolism. Flags were said or imagined to be dyed with blood, but that fiction relied upon an even more precious red.

Red had been associated with imperial flags for centuries, a link that has drawn a good deal of scholarly attention to the history of crimson standards. In 1930, the jurist and historian Herbert Meyer – another scholar of flags eventually seduced by Nazism – connected them to the earliest trappings of princes,

---
[41] Pacheco, 1649: 400.

Figure 7 A Habsburg soldier cuts a fragment from Bern's banner, in Tschachtlans Bilderchronik, 1470. Zürich, Zentralbibliothek, MS A 120, fol. 68. Photo courtesy Zürich, Zentralbibliothek.

and particularly to the so-called "blood flag," a red banner that he associated with early European sovereignty.[42] Just three years later, Carl Erdmann overturned Meyer's simplistic assumptions about the meaning and origins of red flags, arguing against the hodgepodge of interpretations and symbolism that Meyer had provided. A dubious Erdmann listed all the associations Meyer saw in redness: "blood, fire, gold, war, victory, judgment, death, kingship, world domination."[43] We too insist that color is meaningful yet never a simple language to be deciphered. Color is not merely symbolic.[44]

Erdmann's intelligent rigor holds up today; but without falling into Meyer's trap, we can still acknowledge the variegated cultural associations that red flags carried, particularly with ideas of blood. The bold crimson cross on Milan's white standard was said to represent Christ's own blood; sources relate similar descriptions of the Oriflamme: This "red or vermilion banner represents the blood of our Lord Jesus Christ, which he spilled for us on the holy cross to conquer and keep our justice from the enemy," and an earlier chronicler

---

[42] Meyer, 1930.   [43] Erdmann, 1933–34: 26; Weber, 2011: 10.
[44] Baxandall, 1988: 81; Virmani, 2008: 114–15.

portrayed France's standard desiring human blood, ready to soak up whatever poured from adversaries' wounds.[45] Banners thirsted for the blood that nourished their meaning.

On battlefields, flags coalesced with the bodies that guarded them.[46] France's fourteenth-century standard-bearer had to swear even in the face of death never to relinquish the sign of his lord, a scene included in a French manuscript now at the British Library with the text of the oath included (Figure 8). Such oaths bound most of the flag-bearers of premodern Europe: In this regard, these men became synonymous with the polity they represented. In several places the name for flag-bearer indicated one of the chief officers of state, as it did in various Italian cities (*Gonfaloniere di Giustizia*, the Standard-bearer of Justice) and Swiss Cantons (*Venner*, the Banner-bearer, from *Fahne* or its diminutive, *Fähnlein*). Florence's *Gonfaloniere* will reappear in our investigation of the banner currency of Leonardo da Vinci's *Battle of Anghiari*. The *Venner* became an icon in Swiss and German art, a bold masculine form – as in Albrecht Dürer's famous engraving of 1501 (Figure 9) – who wields the idea of state power in his right hand and defends it with the sword grasped in his left. Some women

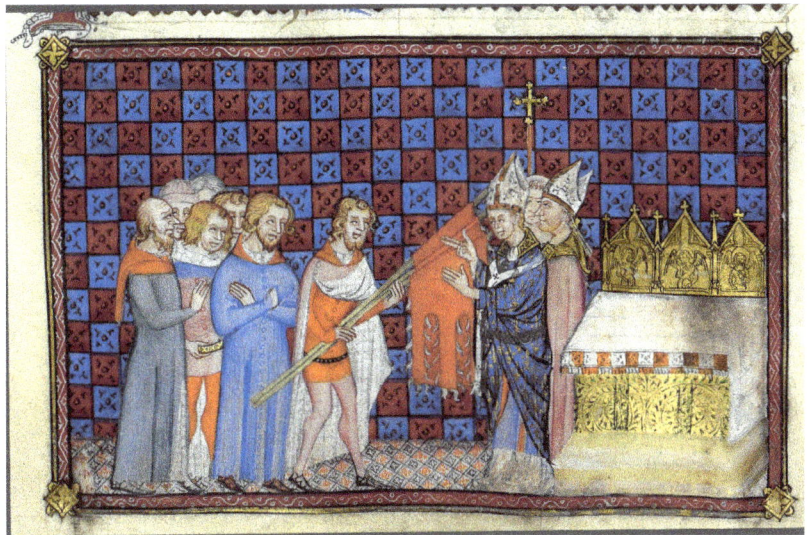

Figure 8 Master of the Coronation Book, the Bishop of Paris blesses the Oriflamme(s), in Coronation Book of King Charles V, ca. 1378. London, British Library, Cotton Tiberius B VIII/2, fol. 73 r. Photo: British Library.

---

[45] For Christ's blood in a fourteenth-century sermon: Erdmann, 1933–34: 38n4. For the Oriflamme: Durand, 1374: fol. 52v. Also, Contamine, 1973: 194, 231.
[46] For complications, however, consider Groebner, 2004: 57, 130, 139.

Figure 9 Albrecht Dürer, the Standard-Bearer, 1500–03. 11.6 × 7.1 cm. Engraving. Washington, National Gallery of Art, 1943.3.3480. Photo courtesy National Gallery of Art, Washington.

claimed this same two-fisted bravado, which is flaunted in a Swiss drawing (ca. 1520) of a barefoot standard-bearer (Figure 10), weighty sword slung around her hips and banner rippling out of frame, an image that may also wink at the stereotypical qualities Dürer invoked.

The French army announced its divine virtue during the Hundred Years War when the virginal Joan of Arc carried her own banner into battle. Joan claimed in her 1431 trial that she loved her banner "forty times more" than her own sword.[47] In her earliest visual representation, a marginal drawing in Parisian parlement records, Joan likewise appears with her blade at her side and a holy pennant held aloft (Figure 11). The parlement clerk here brings them into visual conversation through the parallel horizontal forms of textile and steel. Joan stressed that she carried the banner to avoid having to kill anyone, reminding us that standard-bearers rarely fought but rather guided, making them vulnerable

---

[47] Champion, 1976: 248–9; Contamine, 2007.

Figure 10 Jörg Schweiger (attributed, after Urs Graf), woman with sword and banner, 1520–25. Pen drawing. Basel, Kunstmuseum Basel, Kupferstichkabinett, Amerbach-Kabinett 1662, U.IX.51. Photo courtesy Kunstmuseum Basel.

targets given their precious charge. Typically, however, the standard-bearer was not a chaste teenager but a veteran soldier. Gutierre Díez de Games, one of Joan's contemporaries, bore the standard of his master the Castilian mercenary Don Pero Niño and penned an account of his experiences. In one battle with the English, Gutierre wrote of himself: "[T]he banner and the man who bore it were filled with arrows, as many stuck in his body as a bull has when it runs the ring."[48] Only his armor saved his life. When the French king bestowed the Oriflamme upon its delegated military custodian (the *vexillifer*) for deployment, the soldier had three options: store it in the royal treasury until it was needed, tie

---
[48] Games, 1989: II.lxxiii, 192.

Figure 11 Joan of Arc, in the protocols of Parisian parlement by the clerk Clément de Fauquembergue, 1429. Paris, Archives nationales de France, Registres du Conseil du Parlement de Paris, AE/II/447 (X1a 1481), fol. 12 r. Photo © RMN-Grand Palais/Art Resource, NY.

it to a lance without unfurling it, or drape it around his neck and chest.[49] In wearing the royal banner as a kind of sash or tabard, the *vexillifer* assumed a second skin, the flesh of his lord and the state. To be arrayed in the Oriflamme meant to materialize his oath to give his own blood to defend it.

Swiss chronicles report numerous instances when a flag-bearer fused the flag to his own body in moments of crisis. Many of these tales have the ring of legend, and the first evidence for some appears only several generations later, in the fifteenth or sixteenth centuries. But the coincidence of heroism, self-sacrifice, and flags points to the profound sympathy that bound soldiers to these war talismans. At the Battle of Laupen (1339), fourteen members of the Fülistorff family reportedly perished defending the banner of Fribourg. In the defeat of Bern's soldiers at Laubegg (1342), the banner-bearer Peter Wendschatz, beset by enemies from all sides, launched the banner over the heads of his attackers to assure that it landed safely in compatriots' hands. Diebold Schilling's *Spiezer Chronik* (1484–85) contains a colored pen drawing of Wendschatz, standing tall in the very center of the composition, set to hurl Bern's flag to safety as armored assailants impale him in two directions through

---

[49] Contamine, 1973: 212.

Figure 12 Peter Wendschatz saves Bern's banner at Laubegg (1342), in Diebold Schilling, Spiezer Chronik, 1480s. Bern, Burgerbibliothek, Mss.h.h.I.16, fol. 327. Photo courtesy Bern, Burgerbibliothek.

the ribs (Figure 12). Wendschatz plays the part of a civic martyr, a secular Saint Sebastian pierced by polearms rather than arrows, spilling his own blood to rescue his city's pristine flag. It is crucial to ask: Why did people die for banners? The fact that they did indicates the stakes inherent in their possession and display, and the powerful work that they performed in reinforcing a communitarian ethos. Hardly static symbols, these flags argued for communal belonging and embodied individual sacrifice.

In embellished accounts of the battle at Sempach (1386), the mayor and banner-bearer Niklaus Thut – fearing that the flag of Austrian-allied Zofingen would be seized from him by the Confederates – ripped it to pieces and ate it to prevent its capture. Legend holds that Thut, commemorated in a nineteenth-century monument in Zofingen's main square, was discovered later among the dead, his mouth full of fabric.[50] More than one "banner tale" arose from the

---

[50] There is no record of the flag-eating story before the sixteenth century. See Bickel, 1992: 313–31.

battle at Arbedo (1422), where a Milanese army halted the southerly campaign of Swiss expansion. Peter Kolin died bearing the flag of Zug. His son Johan purportedly grabbed the banner soaked in his father's blood, stripped it from its pole, and wrapped it around his own chest before vaulting himself forward into battle. When Johan himself died moments later, it was only with difficulty that a comrade unbound the flag from his corpse and loosened it from his tight fists.[51] A 1741 catalogue of civic treasures also links a surviving fifteenth-century Nidwalden flag to Arbedo, claiming that the bloodstains of its keeper, Bartholomäus Zniderst, are still visible on the silk taffeta.[52] The potency imputed to banners no doubt encouraged these men to cloak themselves in this second skin, much as they would in armor. The banner's materiality, nevertheless (and hardly surprisingly), failed their bearers, manifesting the fatal gulf between actual fabric and the ideals ascribed to it. These bindings bespeak the protection that the bearer promised to flag and expected from it in return. Extravagant tales of death in defense of heroic flags functioned, most likely, as narrative strategies to explain or vindicate humiliating defeats to posterity.

Such tales illustrate how Swiss banners materialized corporate honor. As tokens of the community, they worked as distillations of esteem or shame. Flags recorded historic moments in material form. Several banners – such as those of Zürich, Basel, Schaffhausen, and Glarus – included long ribbons sewn horizontally along their tops, extending almost twice the length of the flag itself. A bright crimson streamer, for instance, ran atop Zürich's blue and white banner – we see it on the city's early-sixteenth-century banner (Figure 13).[53] These ribbons (*Schwenkel*) belonged to a semiotic culture intertwined with the city's military history. Yet, the rules of this system of meaning were not totally clear or consistent even in the fifteenth century. The ribbons could mark defeat or they could proclaim triumph, and cities sustained divergent stories about their origins.[54] Zürich supposedly attached a "shame streamer" (*Schandzipfel*) to its flag after having lost its battle standard at Winterthur in 1292. While the city's men crumbled on this same campaign, its women, armored and defending Zürich's walls, staved off a planned siege by the Habsburg Duke Albrecht I.

Almost two centuries later, in 1477, Duke René of Lorraine ceremoniously sliced this long-lived strip of dishonorable silk from the flag after Zürchers battled successfully at his side at Nancy. Zürich's guilt had been expiated, and

---

[51] de Vallière, 1908: 619–21, which seemingly relies upon the reports in von Elgger, 1873: 246.
[52] Durrer, 1959: 18–19. See the 1741 catalogue entry reproduced in Bruckner and Bruckner, 1942, Fahnenkatalog (separately paginated appendix to main text): 88–9.
[53] Bruckner and Bruckner, 1942, Fahnenkatalog: 143 (#856).
[54] Neubecker, 1973. For a fourteenth-century "shame streamer": Schib, 1939: 215.

Figure 13 Julius Banner of Zürich with red streamer, 1512. 180 × 367 cm. Silk damask with embroidery. Zürich, Landesmuseum Zürich, DEP-850. Photo courtesy of Schweizerisches Nationalmuseum.

its redemption was dramatically asserted through the prince's gesture, one that understood the flag's material constitution and accretion.[55] Tellingly, the ribbon never disappeared from the Canton's banner but remained a stubborn material insistence of both defeat and victory, the latter only called to mind by the enduring presence of what was eliminated. These fluttering appendages thus not only worked to mark defeat, but in the opposite way as well, to signal imperial favor or some other honor. We must imagine flags as vital statistics, changeable objects whose meanings bespoke the liveliness of corporate fortunes. These streamers remind us too that the visual rhetoric of flags could function in seemingly contradictory – and thus necessarily fluid – ways: Shame and esteem both depended upon military history narratives. This is a far cry from the strict rules regarding heraldic signification that we typically ascribe to this period. Flags were not merely self-evident signs to be decoded.

Tales of sacrifice for the flag, along with their complex language of form, reveal how the Swiss Cantons fused ideological regimes of statehood with embodied performances of self-worth and honor. Swiss chroniclers used a commonplace phrase to describe this fusion: Companies of soldiers always presented themselves for war "with their city banner and full power (*mit ir*

---

[55] Gessler, 1929: 77–8.

statpaner und ganzer macht)."[56] On the one hand, we can see willingness to immolate oneself for a flag as an efficient measure of control that the state could exert upon its soldiers. Notions of corporate pride had been sufficiently instilled to induce fighters to die for their civic symbols, what Ernst Kantorowicz identified as a martyrdom for the political *corpus mysticum*.[57] On the other hand, such cultural investments invite us to refigure the ultimate objectives of military engagement. Certainly, soldiers fought to win battles, but astride victory and defeat rode esteem, for which they continued to struggle even in the face of certain vanquishment. To be despoiled of one's flag materialized defeat because it relinquished honor into the hands of the enemy.

Dynamics of esteem had informed European war-making since antiquity, when stripping civic ensigns cemented ignominious defeats. When ancient Romans conquered illustrious commanders, they paraded the despoiled arms and armor in triumph and displayed them on the Capitol – exuberantly reimagined, for instance, in Andrea Mantegna's monumental canvases depicting the *Triumphs of Caesar*, including men hauling standards, pennons, and banners, along with swords, cuirasses, and helmets. Renaissance Europeans refashioned this ancient ritual by mounting such trophies in churches, which by the fifteenth century were often brimming with weapons and flags, equal parts holy memorials and military prizes. We still glimpse an array of captured banners in the interior of Pisa's church of Santo Stefano dei Cavalieri, decorated with ninety-two standards seized from Turkish navies in the sixteenth and seventeenth centuries, at Lepanto and other battles.[58] The representational value of exhibiting spoils of war (*spolia*) worked in proportion to the opulence of looted military gear: the richer the spoils, the more august the victory.

The Burgundian Wars ca. 1474–77 pitted the Swiss Confederation against the duchy of Burgundy in a dispute over political supremacy of the borderlands between today's France and Switzerland. The sophistication of this military-heraldic culture reveals flags as protagonists in these bloody conflicts, revered objects jealously protected and avidly ransacked. In the series of military defeats that precipitated the ultimate collapse of the Burgundian duchy – at Morat and Grandson in 1476, and at Nancy in 1477 – the victorious Swiss confederacy plundered Charles the Bold's troops of their artillery, weapons, and flags, not to mention the duke's own dazzling encampments, larded with princely goldwork, vestments, tapestries, and household treasures, including a gem one observer called the "largest diamond in the world."[59] The pillage was

---

[56] Bruckner and Bruckner, 1942: 67, quoting from a 1475 Fribourg source.
[57] Kantorowicz, 1951. The related idea of *Todesbereitschaft* (willingness to die) was articulated by Karl Schmitt and summarized in de Wit, 2017.
[58] Nelson, 2016. [59] Motta, 1899.

overseen by nominated Swiss officers: the *Beutemeister* or Booty Masters. Once its troops had safely returned home, each city compiled a register of all the commandeered goods. In Fribourg, they inventoried the spoils man by man: "Pierre Bergo from Treyvaux was chariot-driver of his Company: he found a chest with three men's garments, one embroidered in gold and the two others lined with wolf fur." Or, "Heintzo Wicht of Montablod found 1 dish, 1 paper notebook, and 1 shabby coat."[60] But flying above this ocean of stuff were the most coveted trophies: Burgundy's flags.

From the fields of Grandson alone, the Swiss confiscated over 600 enemy banners, or so wrote the chronicler Diebold Schilling. The number seems immense, but perhaps not exaggerated: Bern's fighters wrote home that they alone had snatched seventy-three.[61] Schilling explained that the flags were numerous and diverse because Burgundian dukes flew the flags of cities and lands they had already subdued in order to "terrify and bring fear" to their opponents in each new encounter.[62] These emblems of past triumph and domination were deployed to terrorize: They threatened future conquest and subjugation. Banners sought to persuade; to elicit powerful emotional and behavioral responses; and to drive citizens and soldiers alike to tremble, submit, or flee.

Loot from Grandson comprised military flags, feudal banners, and ensigns of Burgundy's entire territorial state. The Swiss Confederacy agreed that it would inventory all the flags and then distribute them evenly to the Cantons, in whose cathedrals they would be suspended as trophies. This process of gathering and dividing the flags proved to be contentious, however, as certain cities resisted surrendering tokens they had already mounted in triumph. Splinters in the agreement occurred the following year, when Basel suggested that each Canton should deal with its plunder from Nancy in whichever way it deemed best.[63] Schilling's Bern chronicle illustrates the victorious soldiers carrying flag booty from Grandson and Morat ("there was a lot of it") into the city's Minster to bedeck the nave in triumph (Figure 14). Hanging in Swiss churches and arsenals, the Burgundian spoils attracted glory to each individual Canton, but the "finders keepers" decision to bring these spoils home chafed against the recommendations for equal partition of booty in the long-standing fourteenth-century agreement known as the Sempacher Brief that governed the Confederation's military alliance.[64] No parties wished to relinquish the banners heroically snatched on the battlefield to their confederates, even to foster political unity. These Burgundian flags became such an integral part of each canton's patrimony that, by the time they began to decay in the seventeenth century, several cities

---

[60] Deuchler, 1963: 87–8.   [61] Bruckner and Bruckner, 1942: 75.   [62] Deuchler, 1963: 97.
[63] Bruckner and Bruckner, 1942: 76–81, 92.   [64] Deuchler, 2015: 87.

Figure 14 Diebold Schilling, Amtliche Berner Chronik, 1478–83. Bern, Burgerbibliothek, MSS.h.h.I.3, vol. 3, fol. 829. Photo courtesy Bern, Burgerbibliothek.

commissioned artists to paint miniature copies of them in manuscripts – the so-called *Fahnenbücher*, or Flag Books – to safeguard their still-living prestige (Figure 15).[65] The artists carefully rendered the complex heraldry while observing details such as fringe, gilding, dimensions (with little measuring sticks painted alongside the flags), and even the nails, hooks, or staffs upon which the fabric hung. They had become civic relics: copied with close attention paid to their material form in venues that amplified and distributed their aura and efficacy.

At stake in military representation during the Burgundian Wars was thus a suite of investments: communitarian and affective, organizational and professional, princely and dynastic. At the climactic Battle of Nancy in 1477, these associations collapsed for Duke Charles the Bold of Burgundy. As disorder

---

[65] The genre seems to have emerged with the proliferation of flags: the oldest surviving flag book dates to 1448. Neubecker and Deuchler, 1973.

Figure 15 A Burgundian cornette, in Pierre Crolot, Livre de Drapeaux, 1647–48. Fribourg, State Archives, Législation et variétés 53, fol. 91 r. Photo courtesy Fribourg, State Archives.

reigned near the battle's end, Charles was knocked into a ditch and crushed by a horse. Discovered incapacitated, he died at the hands of Swiss troops who did not recognize him. The Mantuan ambassador wrote that the duke lay there dead for two days, "his head half eaten by dogs."[66] Once the Burgundians recovered his body and returned it to Nancy, they only authenticated the corpse "by a toenail," a forensic scene illustrated in an early sixteenth-century *Songe du Pastourel* manuscript, in which a court page examines the toes of the duke's nearly naked cadaver.[67] (These must be two of the very few bare feet of contemporary noblemen represented in Renaissance art.) Although Charles's remains were rescued and solemnly buried, his anonymous death reveals how efficiently heraldic display produced personhood in the thick of battle – and how easily it could be erased.[68] More than that, the value that disputants accorded to heraldry led them to sublimate the Swiss–Burgundian conflict to a purely representational plane. On the warfield at Nancy, fixation with capturing Burgundian arms ultimately eclipsed the duke who had committed so much energy to their display. As he died anonymously in a trench, his Swiss adversaries despoiled his heraldic gear and absorbed its symbolic and monetary value into their own narrative: They were a coalition of free states repelling princely encroachment. By harvesting Charles's emblems and banners, they both

---

[66] Battioni, 2008: 473.   [67] du Prier, 1500–20: fol. 33r.
[68] See, generally, Groebner, 2004: 12.

castigated princely power and consumed its charisma. Charles the Bold's despoiled flags would help to sustain this cult in Switzerland for the next several centuries.

A splendid system of decorated flags governed the Burgundians' complex military hierarchy, and a novel organizational model augmented their regimented brilliance. The army's central structural units were the large companies (*compagnies*) under the command of a ducally nominated captain. Those companies in turn divided into four equal squadrons (*escadres*) made up of four further subdivisions (*chambres*).[69] One company thus consisted of sixteen chambers in four squadrons, or about 560 men, including archers.[70] In Charles the Bold's Burgundy, banners not only regulated and ordered the troops marching behind their leader (companies fell in line behind the *enseigne* of their captain, who in turn followed the duke's own standard), they also articulated the division of military companies into quarters and sixteenths. Each captain's *enseigne* determined the color and design for his entire company. The company's four squadrons raised flags named *cornettes*, "the first of which is painted with a large golden C," the 1473 Ordinances demanded, "the second with CC, the third with CCC, and the fourth with CCCC." These subdivisions carried on in the flags called *banerolles* that governed the four *chambres*: C i, C ii, C iii, C iiii; CC i, CC ii, CC iii, CC iiii, and so forth.[71] One such *cornette* appears in Pierre Crolot's 1648 catalogue of Fribourg's captured flags (Figure 15). Flags, of course, oriented and directed warriors in battle. Yet, company *enseignes* also invited fighters to bond with them through images of holy figures, such as Saints Anne, Jude the Apostle, Christopher, John, George, Stephen, and others.[72] The desire to safeguard and defend the likeness of the company's patron protector made these standards not just tools of strategic organization but of affective unity and shared identity as well.[73] Martial training exercises further reinforced such sentiments. Of the three war games that Duke Charles recommended for drilling troops, the third involved "running energetically to keep their standards."[74] He knew that conflict might culminate in a tussle for these totems on the move.

Like their Swiss neighbors and rivals, the Burgundians attributed profound representational power to the bearers of flags as princely avatars and as magnets of military attention. For the chamberlain Olivier de la Marche – who himself

---

[69] *Règlement*, 1473: fols. 3r-4r.   [70] Contamine, 1972: 486.
[71] *Règlement*, 1473: fols. 9v, 10r.
[72] Bruckner and Bruckner, 1942, Fahnenkatalog: 164–5 (#1045–49); Deuchler, 1963: 234–70.
[73] Jones, 2010: 11–32, for strategic organization; Virmani, 2008: 86–220, 310, for emotional resonance.
[74] *Règlement*, 1473: fols. 25v-26r. Other training methods were armed war games and running the lance.

led some of Charles the Bold's companies in the 1470s – the ideal ducal equerry incarnated bodily strength, sagacity, justice, fortitude, and daring. To la Marche's mind, a chief duty of the equerry involved "carrying the governing prince's standard, the *enseigne* that is always held up and seen, that everyone follows, that rules over everyone, and to which everyone rallies. [...]The [lesser] *enseignes* owe reverence to the standard, like small sea boats owe to a carrack or a great ship." Likewise, banners of a vassal flew in service of the prince's flag "to show that [the vassal] served in person, and that he wished to keep his faith and loyalty, that he wished to live and die with his prince, as is his duty."[75] In his battle plans for the confrontation at Morat in June 1476, Duke Charles figured the ducal standard as a kind of barge, an immense and unassailable beacon flying above masses of the most elite fighters, a cousin to the French Oriflamme. The Burgundians arrayed eight successive waves of battle lines at Morat, the second of which gathered the duke's gentlemen under the banner of Burgundy (*bannière*) and his own personal standard (*pennon*). At the moment these flags unfurled ("in the name of God, of Our Lady, and of Saint George"), combat began in earnest, and a company escorted the banner to the flank of the duke's closest guards, where it would then direct the army.[76] The banner actuated rather than merely adorned conflict. As the Castilian standard-bearer Gutierre Díez de Games put it: "[T]he banner is like a torch in a room that illuminates everyone; if it happens to be extinguished, all are plunged into darkness, and there lies defeat."[77]

The art of deploying and following an entire theater of airborne signals grew more complex over the fifteenth century as the personnel serving on European battlefields shifted. The growth of professionalized infantry companies, funded both privately and publicly, transformed battlefield signification.[78] The centrality of a commander's personal heraldic banners made new space for those of the units fighting under him. Military strategy now demanded further functionality from silk ensigns governing a proliferating throng of bodies trying to survive a melée of swords, horses, cannons, arrows, pikes, and handguns. The Burgundian Wars came in the midst of this shift, a moment in which we must imagine the battlefield rippling with standards both patrician and plebeian, dynastic and professional, personal and corporate, equestrian and infantry. It is a chapter in the history of choreography and semiosis as much as in the history of war. Like the dance of death, flags broadcasted that the entire society was involved in the conflict, from prince to peasant. At the same time, flags often

---

[75] de la Marche, 1888: 4: 60.
[76] de Gingins la Sarra, 1858: 2: 161. On banners and their proper bearers in these wars: Léderrey, 1962: 370–1.
[77] Games, 1989: 193.   [78] Contamine, 1972: 252.

Figure 16 Bern's black bear attacks Burgundian soldiers at the Battle of Nancy (1477), in Diebold Schilling, Amtliche Berner Chronik, 1478–83. Bern, Burgerbibliothek, MSS.h.h.I.3, vol. 3, fol. 846. Photo courtesy Bern, Burgerbibliothek.

told specific tales about their people's war-like characteristics, and these stories sometimes even came to life. In 1477, the soldiers of Bern – whose flag depicts a rampant bear – loosed a real black bear onto the battlefield to maul their Burgundian opponents (Figure 16).[79] This attack-bear reminds us that heraldry was not merely emblematic, but distilled atavistic powers and cosmic or animal spirits that fighters conjured and deployed in ferocious conflict. The beast could reemerge from the banner and make good on its primeval menace.

In like fashion, the Riminese engineer Roberto Valturio recommended the depiction of fearsome animals on standards in his *De Re Militari* (1472), centuries after Gerald of Wales, ca. 1200, had commented that "fierce and ferocious" bears, leopards, and lions decorated princes' banners "as an index of their own ferocity" and to "strike terror into the enemy."[80] Even for animals merely represented on standards, and not literally embodied, savage animation was still key to their efficacy. Thus, the fourteenth-century jurist Bartolo da Sassoferrato recommended "gnashing teeth and clawing feet" for beasts on banners, specifying they should face the staff so that they would seem to stride forward once enlivened by the wind.[81] Flag and beast: united in the hunt for their human prey.

3 Makers

Burgundian flags survive throughout Switzerland, where they have belonged to civic collections for over five centuries. It is an unusually extensive and variegated patrimony of Renaissance textiles, and one that allows us to look closely at an array of objects, to examine their materiality and think through their making and the sensory phenomena that they activated. Even if many banners have partially disintegrated, they still bespeak their erstwhile beauty, and we can well imagine them whipped up by the wind and electrified by the visual effects of gilded or silvered surfaces. They were adorned with skillfully rendered forms, witty and illusionistic representations of saints, beasts, emblems, and marvelous foliage. This section investigates the painters and artisans who made flags, focusing both on the privileges that accrued with the commissions and the visual rhetorics that artists deployed on these dynamic painted surfaces.

One standard of Duke Charles the Bold now in Zürich consisted of thin silk sturdied with a ground of ocher, white lead, and hide glue (Figure 17). Silver and gold leaf, now corroded, gave the flag its shimmer.[82] Other extant banners display some original brilliance in the dynasty's flame-throwing heraldic

---

[79] Meyer, 1998: 219. [80] Valturio, 1483: fols. E5v-E8r; Jones, 2010: 29; Borgo, 2017: 141–2.
[81] Rihouet, 2021: 612–13. [82] Mäder, 1994.

Figure 17 Banner of Charles the Bold, 1470s, with current deteriorated state on left and artist's reconstruction of original appearance on right. Painted silk. Zürich, Landesmuseum Zürich, KZ-5734. Photo courtesy of Schweizerisches Nationalmuseum. Reconstruction by Sabine Lange, published in Mäder, 1994: fig. 3.

Figure 18 Pennon with Je lay emprins motto of Charles the Bold, 1460s-70s. Paint and gold leaf on silk. Bern, Bernisches Historisches Museum, H/16/c. Photo © Bern History Museum, Bern. Photograph Stefan Rebsamen.

firebrands and Saint-Andrew's cross, and in the lacy gilded lettering of the duke's military motto of the 1470s, *Je lay emprins* or "I have dared it." Six rectangular, sky-blue silk pennants surviving in Bern (Figure 18) feature the phrase *Je lay emprins* in blocky and modeled gilt letters flanked by Charles's emblems of sparking flints. One of the illuminated Swiss chronicles shows what became of these Burgundian pennons when collected as booty. We see them hanging in a chamber amidst other golden trophies: a fur-lined jacket, coins, vessels, a dagger, a ring, and a necklace.[83]

---

[83] Deuchler, 1963: 28.

Figure 19 Burgundian standard of John the Evangelist, before 1476. Solothurn, Museum Altes Zeughaus, MAZ 1135. Photo Nicole Hänni.

An imposing banner taken by Swiss troops at the Battle of Grandson in 1476, a fragment of which survives in Solothurn, confirms the remarkable naturalism and artistic skill that banner-painters showcased (Figure 19). A monumental John the Evangelist displays a basilisk in a chalice, surrounded by Burgundian symbols, including Charles the Bold's C initials and igniting flints. Though the pennant is lavishly gilded (and much restored), subtle shading and cross-hatching render the seated Saint John three-dimensionally, an effect extended to the branch-like cross of Saint Andrew and the chunky metal flints. Even more glistering was a gilded silk taffeta banner's radiant sun – with a pacific, full-lipped face painted on the gold ground – that Count Johannes von Sonnenberg lost two decades later at the Battle of Dornach (Figure 20).

Painters of banners on both sides of the Alps were well-rewarded artists whose commissions often provided not just a livelihood but also civic honor and public offices. The painter-valets Jehan Hennequart and Pierre Coustain appear in the Burgundian court's account books for a variety of armorial paintings in the late 1460s. Hennequart earned thirty-six *livres* for decorating a large white taffeta ducal standard painted on both sides with "the image of our lord Saint George on horseback, combatting the dragon, with the motto and device of our

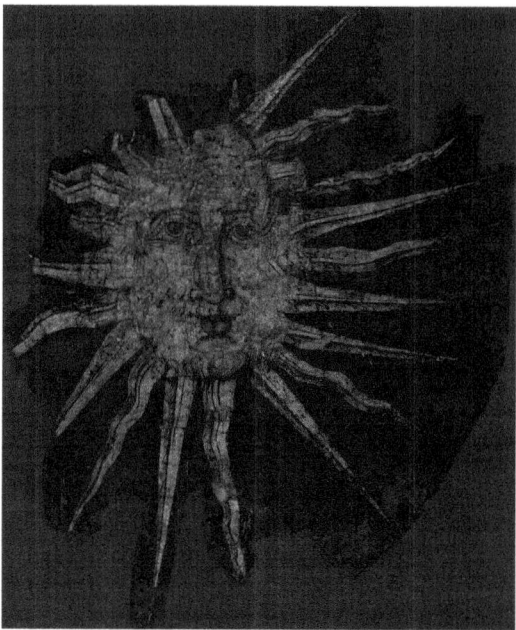

Figure 20 Painted silk taffeta banner, ca. 1490. Zürich, Landesmuseum Zürich, KZ-5725. Photo courtesy of Schweizerisches Nationalmuseum.

Lord the Duke in gold."[84] Though it was painted a few years later, a large, profusely gilded pennant now in Solothurn recalls this banner in both iconography and surface effects (Figure 21); it was seized by the Swiss at the Battle of Nancy in 1477, where Charles met a miserable end. The pennant's tapering triangle stretches nearly ten feet, and its painter maximized every square inch. George, in shining armor and standing upright in the stirrups of his rearing horse, spans the banner's tallest point as he reaches skyward, winding up to smite the splendid dragon with his sword. George's cape, whipping in the wind and in the saint's twisting torsion, leads the viewer's eye diagonally toward his adversary. The creature's little paws desperately grasp at the broken lace piercing its throat; its outstretched wings seem to provide some balance for the beast knocked off its feet and rolling around on its rump, precariously positioned on a small patch of turf. George's energized cloak, moreover, conspicuously parallels the narrowing pennant and helps to animate its forms. The depicted textile thus calls attention to the work's vibrant cloth medium. The wiry, wavy forms of George, the horse, and the dragon give way to the calligraphic design of Charles the Bold's motto, as the banner stretches to the

---

[84] Laborde, 1849: 500, 503; Martin, 1939: 91.

Figure 21 Burgundian banner of St George (and detail), before 1477. Solothurn, Museum Altes Zeughaus, MAZ 1145. Photo Nicole Hänni.

right: once again, *Je lay emprins*. The gold letters weave and wind through linear flourishes and threads, with metallic stalk tendrils twisting and shimmering, providing a moving dynamism that is now flattened on the wall behind protective glass, but must be imagined caught by the wind, its scintillating surfaces lending motion to the warrior saint.

Flag-decorating could pay well: Duke Charles disbursed 600 *livres* in 1472 to Jehan Hennequart for painting "standards, banners, pennons, guidons, and cornettes," a fee surpassing a decade of daily pay for a laborer.[85] Moreover, these were important civic commissions produced by clever, skilled artists, long

---

[85] Martin, 1939: 91.

Figure 22 Agnes van den Bossche, Maid of Ghent, 1481–82. Oil and gold leaf on linen with silk fringes. Ghent, STAM Citymuseum, 00787. Photo: STAM Citymuseum Ghent.

overlooked by art historians. A spectacular banner representing the Maid of Ghent accompanied by a lion, in fact, may be the only documented, surviving painting by a fifteenth-century Flemish woman (Figure 22). This massive pennon – some nine feet wide, painted on both sides – seems to be one of the two linen flags that Ghent's civic government commissioned Agnes van den Bossche to paint in 1481–82. Both depicted the Maid of Ghent and were adorned with green fringes. They served as battle standards for the town's militia of artisan guild members.[86]

Ghent's political culture was saturated with flags. Guildsmen were required to assemble under their banners in the town's Friday market as a regular demonstration of civic accord and of political and military might. Deviations from this custom generally foretold social conflict. When Gentenars conspired against Duke Philip the Good of Burgundy in the early 1450s, their rebellious acts included marching under the prince's banner, hoping to legitimize their cause through the display of his flag. They failed, ultimately, and when the town literally begged the duke for mercy, some 2,000 leading citizens dressed only in undergarments knelt before Philip just outside the city walls. A central aspect of this remarkable ritual was the surrender of Ghent's civic and guild banners, an act represented in a contemporary manuscript illumination. Straightaway the relinquished flags served the Burgundian state as symbols of conquest. The duke's retinue raised them in the vanguard of his parade as he departed Ghent, and they were soon enshrined in cathedrals across his realm.[87]

---

[86] Wolfthal, 1985.   [87] Arnade, 1994.

The banners were replaced in subsequent decades, which brings us back to Agnes van den Bossche, daughter and sister of professional painters. Agnes became an independent master following the death of her husband, and she received numerous commissions for banners and other painted textiles, including trumpet pennons; square, diamond, and cross-shaped flags for triumphs and other civic celebrations; and the canopy for the Virgin of Tournai cult statue, a prestigious commission awarded to Agnes three times, signaling a high level of professional esteem.[88]

The lion that Agnes painted on the surviving banner adorned Ghent's coat of arms and in a late-fourteenth-century poem protects the Maid, a figure for the besieged city (and the gilded fanciful G also stands for Ghent). Her gown of gold-brocaded crimson silk is belted high and tight. Rich ermine fur and tails line the upper hem and complete the dress from the knees down. An intricate necklace frames her delicately rendered face, and her long hair cascades freely, unlike the covered tresses of married women. The Maid and lion stand on a green patch of grass, and with a patting gesture, the Maid seems to calm the king of beasts, who is regally outfitted with a golden crown and bejeweled collar. Agnes animates the forms represented here, responding to the heraldic ornamentation and to the unfurled banner's anticipated motion. The lion's fantastically curling tail, fit carefully within the tapering triangle, flutters and waves like a banner would. Like Saint George's cape, the lion's tail underscores the medium's movement. Agnes's subtle white oil highlights, most noticeable where the beast's tail flowers up in the center, enliven both the creature and the flag itself. Close looking at the *Maid of Ghent* reveals a talented artist well attuned to the object's purpose, promoting a visual banner intelligence that reiterates the image's activation through motion.

Art historians' neglect of these objects arises in part from their classification as ephemera produced by nameless artists, a consequence of tenacious hierarchies elevating painting and sculpture above those quarantined as the decorative or applied arts. Thanks both to feminist scholars centering overlooked women artists of the past and the recent material turn bringing critical attention to a much wider array of textile arts, we are better positioned to appreciate Agnes van den Bossche's monumental and captivating *Maid of Ghent*. But much remains to be done to understand the work of banners in Renaissance culture and the part that artisans played in imagining and producing them.

The *condottiere* Micheletto Attendolo Sforza had a standard of white, green, and crimson taffeta made in Florence by a certain Mattia di Luca *setaiolo* (silk worker) in 1441. Micheletto also ordered a brocaded sack to protect the flag.

---

[88] Wolfthal, 1985; Wolfthal, 1989: 50.

This banner's emblems, or perhaps another's, were painted by Pesello *banderaro* (banner-maker, also sometimes *banderaio*), the maternal grandfather who raised the better-known artist Pesellino.[89] Pesello produced flags for powerful Florentine guilds, the Medici family, and lords, including Guidantonio Manfredi of Faenza and Francesco Sforza.[90] To make banners, painters and embroiderers labored in cooperation with silk workers and gold beaters, and *banderari* like Pesello must have been skilled in several media and materials. Lightweight fabrics like sendal and taffeta, and to a lesser extent plush and textured velvet, seem to have been the most frequently utilized silks. In his early fifteenth-century *Libro dell'arte*, Cennino Cennini provided instructions for preparing sendal banners to be painted and gilded, by laying down gesso, glue, and bole, much like readying panels lined with linen. Banners should be specially varnished since "sometimes they are carried outside when it is raining." Additionally, for standards painted on both sides (as numerous surviving examples are), Cennino recommended drawing the design in white or black chalk reinforced with ink or pigment. Next, he advised, stretch the sendal like a screen in the sun, so that the image's outline is visible through the silk and can be easily traced on the opposite side.[91]

The best known and most studied category of Renaissance banners – Italian ecclesiastical *gonfaloni* – have garnered recognition because they were decorated by a who's who of painters: Andrea del Castagno, Antonello da Messina, Botticelli, Perugino, Raphael, Titian, and Giorgio Vasari, among others. As Pascale Rihouet and Jessica Richardson have shown, *gonfaloni* amplified local cults and devotions, consolidated civic identity, protected the faithful from outbreaks of the plague, and enlivened ritual spaces and moments.[92] Piero della Francesca – whose frescoed battle scenes at San Francesco in Arezzo reveal an attentiveness to the dynamic motion of military standards – produced two confraternal banners in the mid-1460s incorporating gold and expensive ultramarine. The first depicted the Holy Trinity and was made for that confraternity in Arezzo. A separate banner on the reverse seems to have been painted by Luca Signorelli, and a century later Vasari made a *gonfalone* to replace it. Piero's contract for Arezzo's confraternity of the Annunciation banner required him to copy its measurements and image from a previous version. When this second *gonfalone* was delivered, local worshippers donated alms "for the love of said banner," as a confraternal scribe records.[93]

These were treasured objects, as were other hangings. Lords throughout Italy covetously collected and proudly displayed the silk, velvet, and sometimes

---

[89] Predonzani, 2010: 152, 196, 202–3.   [90] Even, 1984: 15, 18, 172, 189, 191.
[91] Cennini, 2015: 209–12, 216.
[92] Franklin, 1995; Bury, 2000; Rihouet, 2019; Richardson, 2024.   [93] Banker, 2014: 103–5.

brocaded banners awarded as grand prize in the horse races whose name *palio* derives from these luxury textiles.[94] For the race run on the feast of Saint George in fifteenth-century Ferrara, the creation of the *palio* banner's entire apparatus – the textile's supporting pole along with a painted shield and crest – was granted to a favored artist at the Este court, in some years Cosmè Tura.[95] In fact, the earliest evidence of Tura's activity as an artist is when he appraised the value of gilded and painted trumpet pennons adorned with Borso d'Este's arms produced for Emperor Frederick III's visit to Ferrara in 1451. Five years later, Tura designed a *gonfalone* for the town's tailors' guild. The contract stipulated that he utilize azurite for the background, and that the banner was to depict the Dead Christ, whose head, the tailors insisted, should be tilted toward the ground to emphasize Christ's lifelessness.[96] Guild flags were marched proudly in civic processions, and they tore through city streets during popular uprisings.[97] A rare surviving guild banner is the two-sided standard of Bern's butchers, dated ca. 1500 (Figure 23). Saint Agnes is accompanied by the lamb of Christ, complete with halo and his *labarum* standard of the Resurrection (white with a cross, here with five tails – compare with Figures 5 and 6) held in place by one of the

Figure 23 Banner of the Butchers' Guild of Bern, ca. 1500. Bern, Bernisches Historisches Museum, H/509/1. Photo © Bern History Museum, Bern. Photograph Stefan Rebsamen.

---

[94] McCall, 2022: 41.   [95] Toffanello, 2010: 47–8, 63, 228; McCall, 2023: 80–9.
[96] Manca, 2000: 178, 181–3.   [97] Trexler, 1984; Cohn, 2008: 177–204; Cohn, 2021: 33–48.

creature's front legs and hooves. Flanking Agnes, opposite the lamb, is a large ox, another animal that the butchers knew intimately. Its lack of a halo, and more ominously the two large cleavers hovering above, wittily remind us of the ox's likely fate and the butcher's profession.

In the fifteenth century, the most magnificent spectacle on the Milanese calendar – the feast of Saint George, protector of the Sforza dukes – culminated in the bishop blessing civic banners at the Duomo's altar dedicated to the saint. The day's events consisted of a parade from the Castello Sforzesco to the Duomo, and back, with the lord and his men at arms accompanying the standards: escorting them to the Duomo, attending the benediction, and returning with the banners to the castle.[98] Equally crucial was the cavalcade's imperious manifestation of Sforza military might. Milanese princes paid close attention to the production of their banners. In March 1475, Duke Galeazzo Maria Sforza requested a court official to obtain, for the lord's approval, a sketch for a white and murrey standard, similar to the "one we have given the illustrious Marchese of Monferrato," but with the eagle "resting," perhaps sitting or nesting, rather than standing tall, and with an additional small yet triumphant scene of the Resurrection of Christ at its top. Two days later Sforza approved the design produced by the painter Costantino da Vaprio and ordered the standard made according to Costantino's directions.[99] The lord ensured that the banner's design closely aligned with another one recently gifted to an ally.

Among the viewers carefully watching banners moving through space were of course chroniclers, who were attuned to the appearance and materiality of the flags that accompanied rule.[100] The anonymous *Diario ferrarese* called attention to three "stendardi" processed by nobles on horseback preceding Ferrara's lord, Borso d'Este, during the visit of Emperor Frederick III. These standards – of green and red silk – were adorned with both imperial and Este emblems, and were echoed by many small white banners "signifying joy" borne by Borso's entourage. When Borso's brother Ercole assumed the town's lordship almost two decades later, "the majority of his courtiers" carried "banderoles," now painted with Ercole's diamond device.[101] These smaller, widely distributed handheld pennants attest to the proliferation of the material culture of banners not just in the hands of princes and warriors, but as the apparatus of the Este regime's courtly machine. More crucially, when gifted to and waved by courtiers and adherents, they served to convince subjects of the lord's authority

---

[98] Lubkin, 1994: 214–18; Covini, 2012: 318–25; Frazier, 2005: 153–7.
[99] Porro Lambertenghi, 1878: 128–9.   [100] Cohn, 2008: 177–204.
[101] Pardi, 1923–33: 35–6, 70.

through their abundance, mobility, and reproducibility. Accompanying chants only further charged these moments, enlivening movement through recurrent, collective sounds.[102]

On city streets and battlefields alike, banners were politically charged. So, it should come as no surprise that not only their bearers but even their makers might suffer because of the political arguments flags made, sometimes even dangerous ones. When the Angevin Queen Giovanna of Naples had her husband Andrea, duke of Calabria, assassinated in 1345, suspicious citizens disinterred his body and discovered a noose around his neck, taken as proof of the queen's crime. These men straightaway commissioned a goldsmith to embroider a large banner depicting Andrea's corpse with the noose, and then charged into Giovanna's palace under this very banner. The queen put down the revolt, though Neapolitans unfurled the flag of the hanged Andrea during subsequent popular insurgencies (as we saw in Trieste and Seville, and in Richard Trexler's nimble account of the Florentine Ciompi revolt, banners invigorated acts of rebellion and resistance). The goldworker who adorned the banner, however, paid the ultimate price. Queen Giovanna had him beheaded once she managed to ferret out his identity.[103]

In Rome, artists who devoted their skills to these ephemeral objects include a raft of painters. Cola Saccoccia, an associate of the better-known Antoniazzo Romano (who himself painted a taffeta *gonfalone* depicting Anthony of Padua in oils with ultramarine), was master of the Roman painters' guild of Saint Luke in 1478. Much of Saccoccia's career was built on the decoration of heraldic gear. In 1471, he and a colleague painted thirty-seven flags for Pope Sixtus IV's entry into the Eternal City.[104] In the early sixteenth century, Pietro Busdraga, a Florentine silk merchant and flag-maker for Pope Julius II, rose to become Custodian of the Sacred Palace and the pontiff's personal provisioner and wardrobe master.[105] Close proximity to authority – and thus access to the cultural matrices of corporate and princely representation that fashioned heraldry – characterized the creative environment of many flag-painters. It is no coincidence that the heraldic painters of the Burgundian dukes were typically *valets de chambre* and thus saturated in the prince's aesthetic desires.[106] Armorers might also be expected to produce or procure banners, since flags were often stored in signorial and civic arsenals and were closely aligned with armies. In 1503, Milan's preeminent metalsmith Bernardino Missaglia was ordered to furnish Francesco Gonzaga "two lances with two painted banners, one with a *crosolo* and the pole in our colors, and the other with a gilded 'T' on the banner and with the staff full of golden T's."[107]

---

[102] Cohn, 2021: 33–48.   [103] Cohn, 2008: 184–5.
[104] Müntz, 1882: 97, 268–9; Cavallaro, 1989: 38; Cavallaro, 1992: 54, 113–15; Bury, 2000: 19–20.
[105] Frapiccini, 2013: 49–50, 76–7.   [106] Martin, 1939: 88–91; Wolfthal, 1989: 3.
[107] Bertolotti, 1889: 127.

Tailors, for their part, acknowledged the fussy patchwork of flag-making, as we see in the renowned late-sixteenth-century Querini Stampalia *Libro del Sarto* and the Madrid tailor Juan de Alcega's printed *Libro de geometria*. After dozens of illustrated patterns outlining the complex curves that an outfitter needed to master for doublets, skirts, and hose, Alcega's manual turns to the right-angled bars and squares required for fashioning Spanish war flags. He advised his reader to account even for the tapering of the lances from which most flags would fly.[108] Banner-makers brought a host of skills to bear upon these transmedial objects, from drawing and brushwork to piecing, needlecraft, passementerie, and embroidery: a spectrum of craft spanning the worlds of painters, goldsmiths, and tailors.

4 Anghiari

Flagstaffs functioned as polearms in Renaissance warfare, and they have served as weapons in more recent unrest, including at the January 6, 2021, insurrection in Washington, DC. A violently wielded flagpole animates artist Hank Willis Thomas's *With All Deliberate Speed* (2018), a large screenprint on retroflective vinyl based on Stanley Forman's photograph of the assault on civil rights lawyer Ted Landsmark during an anti-school-desegregation and anti-busing demonstration outside Boston City Hall on April 5, 1976 (Figure 24). To the naked eye, the image appears to be only the US flag and its pole cutting horizontally through a blurred white field, but the spectral light of a cellphone's camera flash on the retroflective surface momentarily reveals the chaotic scene and vicious assault. What for the newspaper photojournalist Forman signified (judging from his title, *The Soiling of Old Glory*) the flag's debasement, for Thomas – whose title invokes the 1955 second opinion of Brown v. Board of Education, the US Supreme Court decision that struck down school segregation – becomes an indictment of American patriotism's affinity with racial resentment and violence, enmeshed with the flag as both literal and figurative weapon.

A flagpole wielded as a weapon during a vicious fight is likewise at the crux of Leonardo da Vinci's *Battle of Anghiari*. Carlo Pedretti emphasized that the central scene – often referred to as the *Fight for the Standard* – depicts the fight *with* the standard, or, more accurately, its pole, as much as the fight *for* the standard.[109] This fresco, conceptualized by an artist well attuned to contemporary military cultures and practices, was intended for the *Sala del Gran Consiglio*, an expansion of the Palazzo della Signoria (or dei Priori, now Palazzo Vecchio) undertaken by Florence's restored republican government soon after the 1494 expulsion of the Medici regime. Accordingly, the room's decoration was intended to celebrate the

---

[108] Alcega, 1580: fols. 89v-91v.   [109] Pedretti, 2006b: 32.

Figure 24 Hank Willis Thomas, With All Deliberate Speed, 2018. Screenprint on retroflective vinyl. Photo © Hank Willis Thomas. All rights reserved. Photographic credit: The Soiling of Old Glory (1976) published by the Boston Herald; photographer: Stanley Forman.

city's pre-Medicean history and military glory through Michelangelo's and Leonardo's scenes of victories won at Cascina against the Republic of Pisa in 1364 and near Anghiari against Visconti Milan in 1440. Many questions remain about these massive works, each intended to span some 8 × 20 meters (or 26 × 65 feet, close to three times the size of Leonardo's *Last Supper*) on, it seems, the room's east wall.[110]

Remnants of Leonardo's fresco have been the target of a determined search in recent decades. Scientists and scholars sharing a rather romanticized notion of hidden Renaissance secrets have been lured, in particular, to the wall behind a painted green banner emblazoned CERCA TROVA ("seek, and you shall find")

---

[110] Ferretti, 2019.

depicted in Giorgio Vasari's *Battle of Marciano* produced in the 1560s with the help of Jacopo Zucchi.[111] Vasari's fresco, however, is vexillologically precise. The *cerca trova* standard echoes those flown by the exile Bindo Altoviti's troops fighting for the Sienese army defeated by Florence at Marciano. These captured green flags were long displayed in the church of San Lorenzo, where they were seen even by Montaigne.[112] Indeed, no traces of Leonardo's fresco have been identified, and Cecilia Frosinini and others have recently argued that he never even began painting on the wall of the Great Council Hall.[113]

Vasari provides the best-known description of Leonardo's *Battle of Anghiari*, highlighting the ferocity and high stakes of the clash for the Milanese standard. Leonardo was

> asked by Piero Soderini, then Gonfalonier of Justice, to do a decorative painting for the council hall. As a start, therefore, Leonardo began work ... on a cartoon illustrating an incident in the life of Niccolò Piccinino, a commander of Duke Filippo [Visconti] of Milan. He showed a knot of horses fighting for a banner (*bandiera*). ... In the drawing, rage, fury, and vindictiveness are displayed no less in the men than in the horses, two of whom with their forelegs interlocked make war with their teeth no less fiercely than their riders battle for the *bandiera*, the staff of which has been grasped by a soldier who, as he turns and spurs his horse to flight, is trying by the strength of his shoulders to wrest it by force from the hands of four others. Two of them are struggling for it with one hand and attempting with the other to cut the staff with their raised swords; and an old soldier in a red biretta roars out as he grasps the staff with one hand and with the other raises a sword and aims a furious blow to cut off the hands of those who are gnashing their teeth forcefully and ferociously defending their *bandiera*.[114]

Like Vasari, who wrote more than a century after the fact, contemporary accounts emphasized the ritualized contention for banners in combat – much like the Florentine domestic panel paintings we will encounter shortly. The battle took place in late June 1440, on the plain between the Tuscan towns of Anghiari and Sansepolcro, which the Visconti then occupied, near a contested, strategically important bridge over the Tiber River. Control of the bridge changed hands multiple times during the day. Leonardo, art historians think, utilized the bridge to organize his planned composition, by dividing at least two of the expansive fresco's intended three scenes.

Giampaolo Orsini led Florence's troops. He was accompanied by forces directed by Francesco Sforza and his cousin Micheletto Attendolo, in addition to Eugenius

---

[111] Hatfield, 2007; Corazzini, 2023.   [112] Musci, 2011; Corazzini, 2023: 173–6.
[113] Barsanti et al., 2019. See, too, however, Borgo, 2017: 103–6; Bambach, 2019: 2: 364–8; Borgo, 2023; Corazzini, 2023: 76–81, 176–7; Campbell, 2025: 60–5.
[114] Vasari, 1879: 41–2; Fehrenbach, 2007: 400.

IV's papal soldiers under the command of the Patriarch of Aquileia, Ludovico Scarampi Mezzarota (also known as Ludovico Trevisan), who until late 1439 had served as Archbishop of Florence and who would be elevated to cardinal after the battle.[115] The Florentine war commissioners Neri Capponi and Bernardo de' Medici fought as well. On the opposite side, the celebrated *condottiere* Niccolò Piccinino commanded Filippo Maria Visconti's army, supported by captains including Astorre Manfredi (lord of Imola, imprisoned by Florence at Anghiari and then held captive in the Stinche prison) and Rinaldo degli Albizzi, who led Florentine exiles. Niccolò's adopted son Francesco Piccinino also opposed Florence, as he had eight years prior at the Battle of San Romano. There he faced off against Micheletto Attendolo Sforza, his adversary again at Anghiari. In Paolo Uccello's monumental painting of San Romano now in Paris, Francesco rides front and center, with banners and pennants flying above and behind him.

Neri Capponi underscored the centrality of banners for Florence's victory: "[O]ur captain charged from the other side, with 400 war horses, to assault the enemy's standard, and having taken it, they were routed."[116] This war commissioner's summary is as succinct an acknowledgment of the decisive potency of battle standards as any in this study. In a dispatch written at midnight on the day of battle – June 29, the feast of Saints Peter and Paul, to whom the letter-writers attributed this miraculous success – Capponi and Bernardo de' Medici confirmed possession of the precious Milanese "stendardi" and promised to send them home straightaway. They would have delivered banners and letter together, the war commissioners continued, but feared that the prized textiles could be lost. It was vital that the standards arrive in Florence as soon as possible, but they were too important to be carried unprotected, by just any courier. The chronicler Giusto d'Anghiari reported that on the following day news of victory reached Florence. Giusto remarked that the Florentines had snatched the Milanese standards and celebrated enthusiastically, and deservedly so, since Tuscany had been saved.[117] The battle essentially put an end to Filippo Maria Visconti's designs on central Italy.

Across the peninsula – in Bologna, Mantua, Perugia, Rimini, and Venice – chroniclers and correspondents reported the capture of Milan's standards, explicitly linking the act to Florence's triumph.[118] Contemporary literary accounts likewise attest to the salience of Anghiari's banners. The humanist Biondo Flavio asserted that Milanese troops abandoned the flags as they fled. Poggio Bracciolini, in his *History of Florence*, added that "the greater part of the enemies' standards was brought to Florence as testimony of the victory." Leonardo Bruni, moreover, stated that "all the enemy's *vexilla* were seized

---

[115] Cecchi, 1996. [116] Capponi, 1731: Column 1194–5; Masetti-Bencini, 1907: 115–16.
[117] Masetti-Bencini, 1907: 116, 121n83. [118] Predonzani, 2010: 129–31.

and taken to Florence," along with Milanese tents.[119] Leonardo Dati also recorded that Milan's banners were commandeered and carried to Florence in triumph. This source – Dati's *Trophaeum Anglaricum*, a 500-line epic poem in Latin composed three years after the battle – is of particular importance because a vernacular translation and summary made by Niccolò Machiavelli's secretary, the chancery official Agostino Vespucci, was provided to Leonardo as a source for the fresco (penned in the Codex Atlanticus, in Vespucci's hand).[120]

Even voices that do not dwell on the capture of Milanese standards are attuned to the banner culture revealed at Anghiari. An anonymous poet celebrated Florentine men at arms by the thousands like Hector and Achilles carrying "diverse flags of various colors."[121] A poem known as "The Flight of the Captain" narrated the array of standards flown at Anghiari, including those bearing the papal keys, the Visconti viper emblem (*biscione*), and Florence's lily (*giglio*) and lion (*marzocco*). Banners here organized and enlivened soldiers, who, the poet tells us, feared the attack that the sight of flags promised. Victory was secured, in the end, with "3,000 [soldiers] taken and the enemy standards brought down."[122]

The banners confiscated outside Anghiari were promptly exhibited in Florence's two most significant venues. The chronicler Benedetto Dei described "standards of the duke of Milan Filippo Maria," including one of gilded, possibly brocaded, satin depicting the Visconti *razza* or solar emblem, soon hanging above the organ in Florence's Duomo "in perpetual memory and fame."[123] By early 1442, not yet two years after the battle, the flags had been moved to the Palazzo della Signoria. The *Gonfaloniere di Giustizia* displayed in his chamber a white standard with the leopard of Niccolò Piccinino and a crimson flag with the device of the duke of Milan. The two banners are each specifically identified and connected to Piccinino's defeat in additional documents from 1444 and 1458.[124] They remained in the palace at least until 1512, and Leonardo must have had the objects in mind when conceptualizing his intervention in the Council Hall. We should imagine other standards in the space, both Florentine flags and other captured banners. In October 1505, the chronicler Bartolomeo Cerretani recorded that Leonardo had by then begun painting above the seats of the twelve *buonuomini* of Florence's government in the "sala del consiglio." In that room, Cerretani added, hung nine banners taken by Florence a few months prior from Bartolomeo d'Alviano, who led Pisa's troops at San Vincenzo on the Tuscan coast near Elba.[125] Additional artworks intended for the *sala* may have

---

[119] Bracciolini, 1715: 349; Bruni, 1926: 457; Cecchi, 1996: 103–4; Fehrenbach, 2007: 400–401.
[120] Cecchi, 1996: 103; Bambach, 2019: 2: 350–4.   [121] Flamini, 1891: 117–18.
[122] Fabretti, 1842: 250, 258, 266, 272–3, 275.   [123] Dei, 1985: 55–6.
[124] Cecchi, 1996: 104; Rubinstein, 1991: 282n41; Rubinstein, 1995: 73–5, 99; Predonzani, 2010: 123, 129. The leopard is likely instead a cheetah: McCall, 2023: 91–6.
[125] Cerretani, 1993: 115–16; Hatfield, 2007: 1, 5, 36–9; Bambach, 2019: 2: 363–4, 385.

conspicuously featured banners: the *Risen Christ* commissioned from the sculptor Andrea Sansovino; Fra Bartolomeo's unfinished altarpiece depicting, among Florence's patrons and protectors, Saint Victor holding a banner; and even Michelangelo's *Battle of Cascina*, won in 1364 on Victor's feast day, which Michael Cole surmises may have been planned to include a soldier raising a standard.[126] Banners – real and represented, looted trophies and Florentine treasures – festooned the new hall of state, thematically unfurling from Leonardo's fresco and literally hovering above the town's powerbrokers.

The presence of Milanese standards in Florence's Council Hall would have amplified the banner politics activated by Leonardo. Some scholars have argued that the *Battle of Anghiari*, by spotlighting a small number of *condottieri*, glorified heroic foreign mercenaries. Others claim that the scene should be read in an opposite manner, supporting Machiavelli's ambitions to raise a standing Florentine militia.[127] In both interpretations, the dramatic representation of a violent clash over a banner would have intensified Florentine republican patriotism and loyalty to the flag, and by extension to the office and person of the *Gonfaloniere di Giustizia*, Piero Soderini, recently appointed to this post for life and the motivating force behind Leonardo's commission.

Leonardo worked in Florence on the project from October 1503, when he was given keys to the *Sala del Papa* and other rooms at Santa Maria Novella, until May 1506, when he was granted permission to depart for Milan for three months. In a letter to the French king's representative there, Piero Soderini lamented that Leonardo had been paid a considerable sum but had only accomplished "a small beginning on a large work."[128] Already in October 1503, the chancery official Vespucci – in a dated marginal notation in his printed copy of Cicero's *Epistulae ad Familiares*, in which he also provided the first known identification of the *Mona Lisa* with Lisa del Giocondo – voiced skepticism that Leonardo was up to the task for the fresco "in the Hall of the Great Council, now that he has made an agreement with the *Gonfaloniere*." Though busy with the *Mona Lisa* and other works in these years, Leonardo dedicated himself to the Anghiari project; Carmen Bambach recently wondered if the "fiery intensity and labor" of his many sketches and drawings ultimately sapped his "creative energies," leaving Leonardo overwhelmed by the immensity of the fresco.[129]

The brutal crush of colliding horses and warriors that scholars and students know as the *Battle of Anghiari* would have occupied perhaps a third of Leonardo's fresco. The *Fight for the Standard* comprised the central of three

---

[126] Cole, 2014: 22–3.
[127] Rubinstein, 1991; Cecchi, 1996; Fehrenbach, 2007: 401–2; Musci, 2011: 257–8.
[128] Melani, 2012: 29–33; Bambach, 2019: 1: 25; 2: 252–3, 359–62, 369; 3: 89, 317.
[129] Borgo, 2017: 98; Bambach, 2019: 1: 25; 2: 347–9, 356, 416.

episodes from the battle, laid out in a unified horizontal landscape, the whole of which art historians have sought to reconstruct from Leonardo's drawings and other visual evidence. It seems that the fresco's far left would have depicted horsemen charging toward the center, while at right, additional mounted soldiers clashed near a bridge, with flags flying (Figure 25).[130] Insight into Leonardo's shifting designs for the *Fight for the Standard* are provided by several surviving drawings, some with fluttering banners, in addition to what we can reconstruct of nonextant works in Leonardo's hand: the large cartoon, plus likely a second cartoon, for transfer, according to Bambach's analysis of Leonardo's paper purchases; a sketchbook that in the Madrid notebooks he called a "book of horse drawings for the cartoon"; whatever was drawn or painted on the wall; and a small trial painting testing one of Leonardo's novel techniques in oil. Glimpses are likewise offered by a cluster of painted, drawn, and engraved copies – but this group of images shares an immensely complicated history and chronology that scholars cannot fully parse. It is exceedingly difficult to discern how they revise, respond to, duplicate, or adapt previous reproductions, let alone Leonardo's own works and ideas.[131]

The banner itself is absent from many versions and copies of the *Fight for the Standard*, though its staff is often prominently represented. The pole, in fact,

Figure 25 Leonardo da Vinci, study for right side of the Battle of Anghiari, 1503–04. Black chalk. Windsor Castle, Royal Library, 12339 r. Photo © Royal Collection Enterprises Limited 2025 | Royal Collection Trust.

---

[130] Hochstetler Meyer, 1984: 367–81.
[131] Joannides, 1988: 76–86; Zöllner, 1991: 177–90; Bambach, 1999; Melani, 2012: 49–89, 105–15; Bambach, 2019: 2: 368–80, 385–416; Barsanti, 2019: 315–32.

serves as a pivot activating Leonardo's mechanics of force, resistance, and movement.[132] Raphael's early silverpoint drawing in Oxford – a tiny sketch based on one of Leonardo's lost drawings or cartoons – emphasizes the staff, from which waves a flag that at the same time approximates the horseman's mantle flapping in the wind (Figure 26).[133] Other artists likewise conflated the standard with a flowing cape, and many depicted the staff breaking once, or even twice. Rubens reinstated the standard at the battle's center in what is now the most familiar stand-in for *The Battle of Anghiari* (Figure 1). Rubens' Louvre drawing is, in fact, a slightly enlarged and very energetic reworking in pen, wash, and lead white of a sixteenth-century sketch by an artist close to one of Leonardo's original designs. It is perhaps the most dramatic of the early modern renditions of the *Fight for the Standard*, indebted to Vasari's harrowing account of the taut, violent action.[134]

Viewers have endeavored to make sense of Leonardo's tangled mass of warriors. Giorgio Vasari identified the two on horseback at left as Florentines, one turning towards us, and through this pivoting torsion attempting to ride away with the staff, while his comrade raises his sword to cut off the hands of those defending it (and remember that Dante in *Inferno, canto* 32, banished the traitorous Bocca degli Abati to hell for severing the hand of the Florentine standard-bearer at the 1260 Battle of Montaperti, leading to Florence's defeat). The consensus of modern scholars, however, sees Florentines as the warriors to the right, for they seem to carry away the standard in certain copies, including Rubens'. Giampaolo Orsini, Florence's captain, may face off here against Niccolò Piccinino. Their steeds collide face to face, as Vasari put it, "a knot of horses fighting for a *bandiera*" who "make war with their teeth." Orsini reaches out from the right and grasps the staff, while Piccinino ferociously shrieks with sword raised.[135]

Preparatory drawings of these howling men indicate just how crucial the representation of their desperation, determination, and agony was to Leonardo. His black chalk study in Budapest of the battle-weary Piccinino and another artist's later reworked and expanded depiction of his head (transferred from Leonardo's first cartoon since traces of *spolvero* can be discerned) convey the moment's vicious drama and intensity.[136] In later printed and drawn reinterpretations, an end of the broken staff has morphed into a lance or spear, its blade-tip threateningly directed at Piccinino's face and eyes. The central Milanese

---

[132] Cole, 2014: 112–15, 130–3. Also, Cederlöf, 1959: 98.
[133] Joannides, 1988: 77–9; Bambach, 2019: 2: 354, 362.
[134] Zöllner, 1991; Barone, 2009: 443–7; Bambach, 2019: 2: 398–9.
[135] Vasari, 1879: 41; Fehrenbach, 2007: 410; Bambach, 2019: 2: 370, 379, 406–10.
[136] Barone and Kemp, 2019.

Figure 26 Raphael, sketch after Leonardo's *Fight for the Standard* (from page with studies for Holy Trinity with Saints in San Severo, Perugia), ca. 1505. Silverpoint. Oxford, Ashmolean Museum, KP II 535 (WA 1846.176). Photo © Ashmolean Museum, University of Oxford.

warrior is imperiled as well by a second Florentine wielding a sword (or a battle-axe in Lorenzo Zacchia's unique woodcut print of 1558, the lone securely dated copy). The identification of these *condottieri* is far from definite, however, nor would they have been understood by all early modern viewers, as Vasari's many confusions certainly demonstrate. Indeed, Leonardo accentuated emotional charge and ferocious brutality above narrative clarity – his clash of human and equine bodies entangles into a vortex of metal and fabric.[137] As with the *Last Supper*, copyists were often stymied by Leonardo's visual ambiguity and did their best to complete, simplify, and (ostensibly) rectify it.[138]

Leonardo's is the best-known artistic depiction of the Battle of Anghiari, but not the first. Banners propel the visual narratives in a series of paintings dated to the 1460s, including two *cassoni*. One in Madrid's Museo Arqueológico Nacional incorporates a front and two lateral panels in a partially nineteenth-century chest; a second *cassone* with paintings compositionally very similar to Madrid's was sold in 1923 and has been subsequently lost to scholars.[139] With banners flying, a furious battle stretches the width of the two *cassoni* fronts, on either side of a lone bridge over the Tiber. Horsemen charge, some tumbling from their mounts, as the Milanese flee toward Sansepolcro, with dead and injured soldiers littering the ground. Florentines proceed in a more orderly fashion into Anghiari, with their leaders decorously arrayed at far right. In the lost panel known through photographs, just right of the bridge, a violent clash

---

[137] Borgo, 2017: 110–12. [138] Steinberg, 2001.
[139] Schubring, 1912; Schubring, 1913; Cederlöf, 1959; Predonzani, 2010: 73–5; Polcri, 2006.

between mounted warriors armed with lances and maces reminds the viewer of a slightly more populated and less compressed antecedent for Leonardo's *Fight for the Standard*.

The combat represented in a third, larger panel in Dublin (perhaps from a wall *spalliera* rather than a *cassone* chest) resounds even louder as a precursor to Leonardo (Figure 27). It is precisely centralized, occupying the entire foreground space between two bridges. Decades ago, art historian Olle Cederlöf recognized features of the Dublin painting's composition as potential evidence that it had informed, if not inspired, Leonardo's conception of the fresco – an intriguing suggestion cited by scholars only rarely, and not taken seriously enough.[140] Cederlöf called attention to the scene's wide, horizontal orientation; its separation into three components by two bridges over the winding Tiber and a tributary;[141] and its front-and-center focus on the battle under the banners, with those of Milan on their way down. Crucially, while banners and their capture are again and again described in fifteenth-century accounts of Anghiari, a brutal fight over them is not. This may have been Leonardo's invention, perhaps in consultation with Soderini, Vespucci, or Machiavelli, or possibly looking at the Dublin panel, at the time displayed in a Florentine palace.

The battle rages within the valley between Sansepolcro and Anghiari, with the Visconti viper or *biscione* above the former's town gate, and the latter surmounted by Florence's lily or *giglio*. The white walls of Città di Castello are visible in the distance. Banners ripple above the melée and appear dispersed across the panel, amidst the crush of warriors, horses, and weapons. Flags also advance the narrative of a companion painting in Dublin depicting Florence's *Taking of Pisa* in 1406, most resonantly above the main gate, where the Republic of Pisa's crimson flag with a white cross is taken down just as Florence's is triumphantly raised and planted (Figure 28). In Dublin's *Anghiari*, our attention is directed front and center, with tenaciously erect Florentine standards on the right, and three Milanese banners to the left, being brought down before our very eyes (Figure 29). Left to right, we see a golden flag adorned with a sitting creature on a darker gold ground, framed by a circle. Its front legs suggest that this is Niccolò Piccinino's griffin insignia, though its body and head seem to depict his leopard, which we know decorated one of the banners carried back to Florence.[142] Just to the right, a white standard bearing the Visconti *biscione* comes crashing down, its staff nearly parallel to the ground.

The third Milanese banner is difficult to discern with its painted or metal surface worn away (as with the armored knights beneath it). It is possible to make out the flag's two flame-like tails fluttering at the back of this mess of yellow and gold,

---

[140] Cederlöf, 1959. Also, Hochstetler Meyer, 1984: 367–71; Dalli Regoli, 2012: 84–5.
[141] Hochstetler Meyer, 1984: 371–2.   [142] Predonzani, 2010: 143–8; Polcri, 2006: 76.

Figure 27 Unknown painter close to Apollonio di Giovanni, The Battle of Anghiari, 1460s. Spalliera? Tempera and gold leaf on panel. Dublin, National Gallery of Ireland, NGI.778. Photo: National Gallery of Ireland.

The Fabric of War 53

Figure 28 Unknown painter close to Apollonio di Giovanni, Men discarding Pisa's flag and planting Florence's, detail from The Taking of Pisa, 1460s. Spalliera? Tempera and gold leaf on panel. Dublin, National Gallery of Ireland, NGI.780. Photo: National Gallery of Ireland.

Figure 29 The central battle with Milanese standards falling (detail of Figure 27). Photo: National Gallery of Ireland.

immediately in front of a soldier bending over to load his crossbow. This is the crimson banner bearing the Visconti *razza* or radiant sun emblem that the Florentines also took home as booty. The abraded, muddled gold on crimson can be identified as the *razza* standard by observing that it is twice flown together with the same pair of banners elsewhere on the panel: in the far distance at left, as Milanese troops assemble outside Sansepolcro prior to battle, and again at upper right, paraded by the Florentines into Anghiari in triumph (Figure 30). Thus, two standards that we know were seized at Anghiari are represented here, portraits of loot depicted within the narrative of their confiscation. The third, the one marked with the *biscione*, is never mentioned in our sources, but its inclusion in the Dublin

Figure 30 Florentines parading Milanese standards into Anghiari with leaders arrayed at right under their flags (detail of Figure 27). Photo: National Gallery of Ireland.

panel can be explained by the fact that it would have been the most familiar Milanese heraldry for the painting's original Florentine audience two decades later.

Above the spirited combat between the two bridges – a mass of a few dozen knights crashing into each other and trampling fallen soldiers and tumbled horses – are three conspicuously upright Florentine banners (a fourth, perhaps depicting a rampant bear of the Orsini seems to be adjacent to these but is carried by a charging horseman in the distance beyond the fray). The three banners overlap, especially the left-most two. Thus, we only glimpse the Sforza flag quartered with crimson branches and yellow quince fruits or *cotogni*, a play on Cotignola, the dynasty's hometown, in addition to the Attendolo Sforza *ondato* emblem, blue waves (now oxidized black) on a white or silver ground. Easier to discern are the crimson banner adorned with the crossed papal keys, associated here with Ludovico Scarampi Mezzarota, and a white standard bearing Florence's red *giglio*.[143] The same three are visible – and more fully legible – above the ranks of warriors arrayed in the right foreground (Figure 30). Particularized faces suggest that viewers may have recognized these portraits as Florentine officials and *condottieri*, including Neri Capponi, Bernardo de' Medici, Micheletto Attendolo Sforza (perhaps the fighter in front grasping the baton of command), and Scarampi Mezzarota, who wears a wide-brimmed cardinal's hat with tassels (the *galero* – here black though traces of paint suggest it was originally crimson). One scholar perceives Cosimo de' Medici in profile just behind these four mounted generals. If this is Cosimo anachronistically witnessing the triumphal parade into Anghiari, it is noteworthy that the Florentine *giglio* pennant whips around to touch his crimson biretta, almost sanctifying the Medici regime through the Anghiari banner cult still alive decades after the battle.[144]

5 Gifts

War booty, and its allure, motivated Leonardo da Vinci and his Florentine patrons, as it did many other players throughout Europe in the years around 1500. As we have seen, the Swiss Cantons in the fifteenth century vaunted captured flags as victory trophies as much as they fervently identified with and defended their own banners as materialized civic regard and masculine honor. One of the most remarkable episodes in Swiss commitment to what we call their banner cult unfolded four decades after the Burgundian Wars, in the early sixteenth century, when the cantonal fighting companies joined the papal payroll during the Italian Wars as a wedge against French rule in northern Italy. Key in soldering Swiss fortunes to the papacy was Matthäus Schiner, Bishop of Sion (1470–1522). He

---

[143] Schubring, 1912: 158; Predonzani, 2010: 151–3; Polcri, 2006: 76.
[144] Polcri, 2006: 76. Also, Predonzani, 2010: 175–6.

orchestrated the alliance with Pope Julius II (r. 1503–12), became papal legate to Italy and Germany, and won a cardinal's hat along the way.[145] In 1510, Schiner put Swiss fighters in the Pope's service for a string of strategically successful battles through mid-1512. After Swiss forces uprooted the French from Pavia in June of that year, Julius awarded the Cantons the perpetual title of "defenders of ecclesiastical liberty" and gifted them the papal sword and hat, a prize accorded annually to the Pontiff's most valiant protector. In addition, "as a sign of their true faith and virtue," Julius gave the twelve Cantons two banners "with the [papal] keys, arms, our crest and that of the church, which they can perpetually use and enjoy."[146] Julius knew how to appeal to Swiss traditions of military self-regard. He understood that for the Swiss in particular, lavish silk flags furnished a supremely cherished currency of glory.[147]

The spring and summer of 1512 were seasons of banner fever. With each Italian city they defeated, the Swiss companies voraciously gathered trophy flags. In a house just outside Pavia, the Fribourg captain Peter Falk described finding a brand-new banner, "more beautiful than any we have in the Confederacy." It was an abandoned equestrian standard for French King Louis XII to fly against the Swiss. Falk now dreamed of hanging it in his home cathedral of Saint Nicolas. Falk sent it, along with seven or eight other banners, to his wife in Fribourg and instructed her in an enclosed letter to open the package in secret, perhaps because his plunder included flags even of allies.[148] In Milan, Matthäus Schiner distributed to the Swiss all the flags that the French had seized from their opponents just three months earlier at Ravenna, which were already bedecking Milanese churches.[149] Schiner arranged for two of the Cantons with the longest pontifical affiliations – Basel and Fribourg – to receive a special gift in Julius's name: a luxurious, papally sanctioned version of their own civic banner decorated with an exquisitely embroidered holy scene in the top corner, sometimes called an *Eckquartier* (corner quarter), a detail particular to Swiss flags, but with precedents that go back at least to Byzantium.[150]

Schiner announced the gift to Basel's army on the evening of July 1, 1512, and the Baslers – camped near Alessandria in the duchy of Lombardy – sent agents to Milan to order their flag the very next day. Army accounts show an expenditure of 52 Kronen, later reimbursed by Schiner. The big-ticket costs included over 11 yards of white silk damask (9 Kronen), ornamental embellishments (8 Kronen), pearls (6 Kronen), the painter's labor (4 Kronen), and the biggest outlay of all: the embroidered scene of the Annunciation (19 Kronen),

---

[145] Büchi, 1923: 279–89, 299–301.   [146] Kaiser, 1869: 633.
[147] Bruckner and Bruckner, 1942: 167.   [148] de Diesbach, 1893; de Vevey, 1943.
[149] Godefroy, 1712: 3: 282.
[150] Durrer, 1905: 121; Durrer, 1907: 286. For Byzantine examples of banner stitchwork: Strohmaier, 2017: 219–23.

almost half the value of the entire commission.[151] This costly and delicately wrought Annunciation *Eckquartier* survives today in the Historisches Museum Basel; it is a jewel of Milanese stitchwork (Figure 31). In a sparkling robe, the archangel Gabriel alights near the frightened Virgin as God the Father, in refulgent clouds, sends Mary a nacreous dove. The panel coruscates with a riot of loops and lines of silken and metallic threads, scores of miniscule pearls, and hundreds of delicate *magete*, the tiny paillettes manufactured in Milan by an entire industry of low-wage workers.[152] Layered atop one another, the sequin-like *magete* provide a glistering frame to the scene. Stitched together and held in place by gilded fibers, they comprise the splendid cloaks of angel and Virgin alike. The artisans who produced this radiant image utilized a variety of metal-sheathed threads and wires to suggest a plethora of visual, material, and surface effects. Note the spaghetti-like brocaded strands of Mary and Gabriel's hair, or the gilded strings emanating from God's mouth and extending through the dove into the top of Mary's head.

Milan sustained a thriving community of embroiderers working for both ecclesiastical and courtly patrons, one connected to the town's booming silk industry, and the Baslers likely made their order in the workshop of one of these masters.[153] In the very same years, the painter Giovanni Ambrogio Bevilacqua and other artisans were experimenting with similar mixed-media compositions – including silk ground, paillettes, and metal-wrapped brocade – for domestic religious panels.[154] This *Eckquartier* epitomizes a particular thread of Lombard decorative arts, one to which Basel's commissioners were doubtless sensitive: The army envoys Jakob Meyer and Hans Oberried were two of Hans Holbein's earliest patrons.[155] Even if most voices in Milan in the 1510s lamented the presence of unruly Swiss troops, these sparkling embroidery commissions represent a rare collaboration between Milanese artisans and the Swiss military to manufacture treasured embellishments. The banners' *Eckquartieren* comprised a crucial aspect of the luxury material culture of Renaissance war and reveal how encampments of soldiers patronized the workshops of skilled textile artisans.

When the Baslers received their finished banner in July, they proudly flew it over their encampment publicly for three days to the sound of fifes and drums.[156] Although Schiner had planned only to endow two Cantons with papal banners, news of the gifts spread quickly, and the cardinal understood that the only way to avoid recriminations was to extend the benefaction to all the Cantons. Gifts, this episode confirms, operated as agents of union that embodied recognition or favor,

---

[151] Durrer, 1907: 285–6. [152] McCall, 2022: 71–4. [153] Buss, 2009; McCall, 2022: 46–53.
[154] McCall, 2018: 252–60. [155] Durrer, 1907: 355. [156] Durrer, 1907: 260.

Figure 31 Annunciation Eckquartier from Julius Banner of Basel (and detail), ca. 1512. Basel, Historisches Museum, 1892.92. Photo © Historisches Museum Basel, Peter Portner.

but they could equally spur disunion and inflame rivalries. In the end, the gift list included not just the core members of the Confederation but additionally all the allied counties and cities, a total of over forty flags, from Appenzell to Zürich.[157]

A number of Julius banners survive with intact *Eckquartieren*, splendid material attachments through which the pope fused his power with Swiss armorial identity. Solothurn has two with embroidered *Eckquartieren* and a third with the scene painted on both sides of the silk. One standard encompasses a band of crimson damask above one of white damask, of about equal size (Figure 32). The silk still shines, and the figured damask remains remarkably legible. The banner's upper-left *Eckquartier*, depicting Saint Ursus kneeling before the suffering Christ, manifests a multi-materiality of gilded silver threads, pearls, small *magete*, a metal star for the knightly saint's spur, and fabric to bulk out the figures.[158] Christ and his devout follower are a meticulously crafted pair. Metal threads provide volume for Christ's

Figure 32 Eckquartier (detail of Figure 34) from Julius Banner of Solothurn, ca. 1512. Solothurn, Museum Altes Zeughaus, MAZ 1108. Photo Nicole Hänni.

---

[157] Bruckner and Bruckner, 1942: 175–99; Rihouet, 2021: 612–14.
[158] Bruckner and Bruckner, 1942, Fahnenkatalog: 110 (#641, 642, 643).

sponge and create Ursus's flag adorned with a cross. The kneeling warrior looks up at his savior with visor raised. Seed pearls circumscribe the halos of both men; they also outline and highlight the knight's armor and Christ's loincloth and crown of thorns. The cords of Christ's flagellum whip in the air, as does his drapery immediately below. Their wave and flutter recall the banner itself, its maker cleverly anticipating and echoing the medium's essential kinetics.

In 1513, Hans Rüegger impressed a woodcut celebrating not just the pontifical banners, sword, and hat but also the Schiner gifts, shown in the fists of sixteen cantonal standard bearers (Figure 33). Rüegger took care to record details of design, cut, and format, not to mention the floriate pattern of the Milanese silk damask that almost all the flags shared. Significantly, the artist made the *Eckquartieren* – the fulcrums of devotional imagery and deluxe materiality alike – much more legible in the woodcut than in the textiles themselves. Solothurn's banner (shown reversed in the print) presents an enlarged, telescoped, and schematized scene (Figure 34). Enlarged because Rüegger's printed *Eckquartier* takes up much more of the banner's upper half than does the actual object. Telescoped because Christ is shown only from the waist up, though the kneeling knight and his flag are depicted in full, compressed within this space. And schematized because the embroidered whip and sponge held upward, made of silk and gilded threads, have been translated by Rüegger from the figurative *arma Christi* into Christ's literal arms, slightly raised and in the same position, thus simplifying a potentially confusing detail in the woodcut. Such differences also remind us that depictions of heraldry are always mediated, adjusted, and revised, and they serve new and alternative representative functions. Still, banners were most efficacious when viewed, and these flags gained new life when they moved beyond the battlefield and found wider audiences in print.

Following this cascade of gifts, Swiss cities that had been left out of papal favor tried to catch up. Gifts solidify alliance, and their lack can conspicuously suggest exclusion, on some occasions exacerbating tensions and jealousies. Troops from the allied city of Mulhouse had fought for Pope Julius II in 1511, but under the banner of Basel, and so Mulhouse received no official recognition.[159] In October 1512, Mulhouse sent Jean Oswaldt-Gamsharst, the city's cleric-syndic, to Rome to request a litany of mundane papal privileges relating to rents and taxes.[160] But his agenda also included a request that Mulhouse's flag be updated and enriched with precious metals: The council members wanted the town's devices fashioned in silver and its watermill-wheel emblem in gold rather than black. They also desired an *Eckquartier* depicting Mulhouse's patron, Saint Stephen, and the whole banner framed in gold branches. On his descent toward

---

[159] Durrer, 1907: 324.   [160] Moeder, 1923.

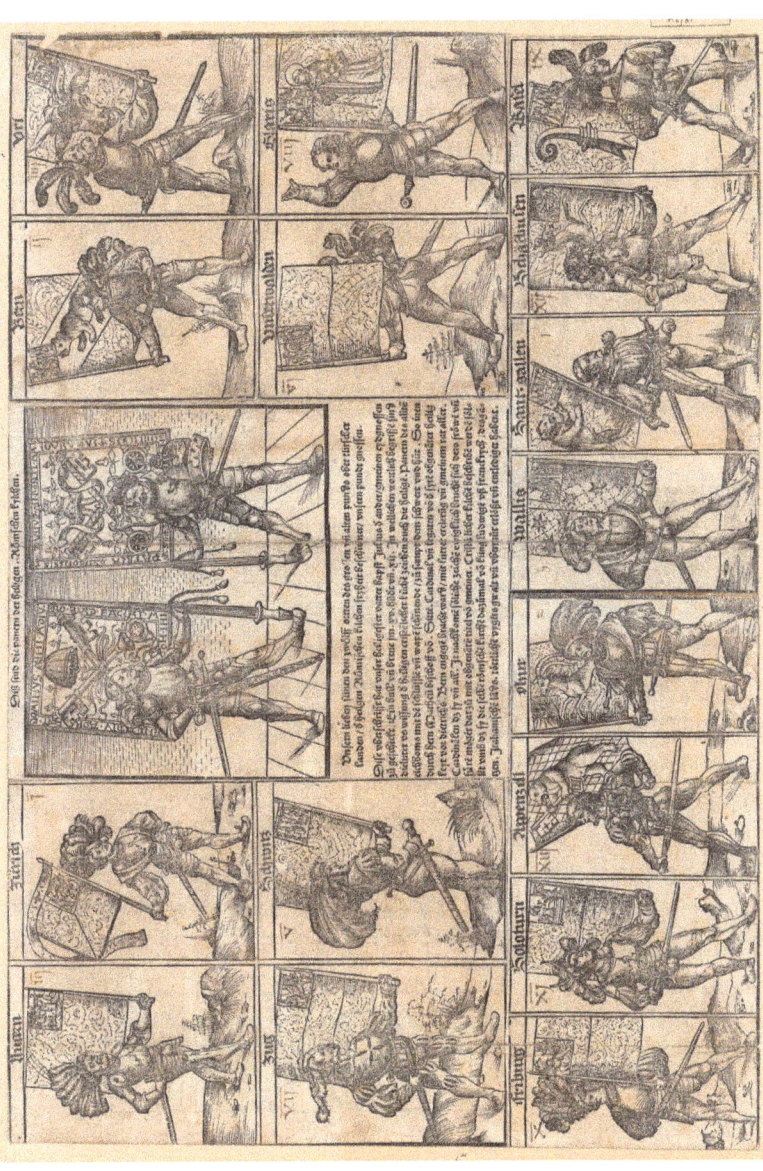

Figure 33 Hans Rüegger, Julius Banners (Wie vnser heiligester vatter bapst den. Xij. ortten d'Eidgnoschafft vnd andern Jre paner mit sunder zeichn des lidens cristi begabt hat), 1513. Engraving. Zürich, Zentralbibliothek, Graphische Sammlung und Fotoarchiv, 3756. Photo courtesy Zürich, Zentralbibliothek.

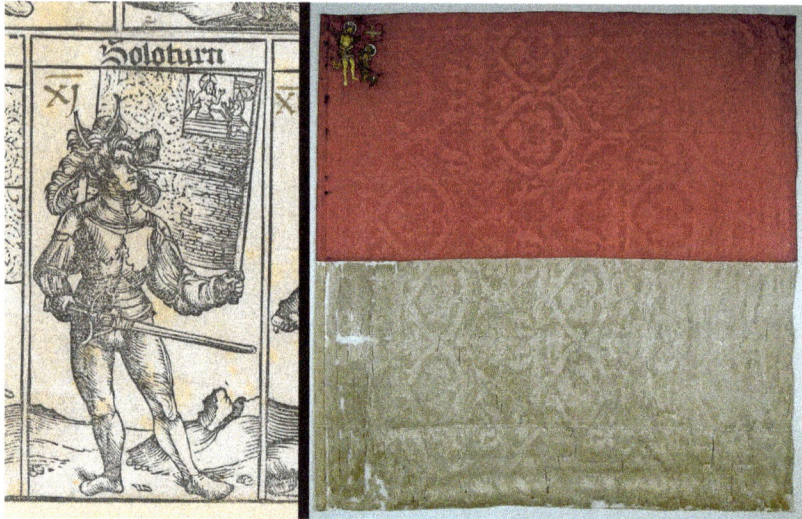

Figure 34 Hans Rüegger, banner-bearer of Solothurn (detail of Figure 33). Julius Banner, ca. 1512. Solothurn, Museum Altes Zeughaus, MAZ 108. Photo Nicole Hänni.

Rome, Oswaldt-Gamsharst had the luck to encounter Schiner in Lodi, and the cardinal ratified the flag request, which the syndic ferried on to Rome.[161] At the papal court, Oswaldt-Gamsharst faced almost total defeat on the policy agenda at the heart of his mission, but the pope agreed to allow Mulhouse to upgrade its banner's millwheel "to a golden and military color." Accordingly, the syndic had a new flag produced, probably in Milan on his return home, with each detail rendered just as the council desired.[162]

In a bull issued in late December 1512, when Oswaldt-Gamsharst was still attending the Roman court, the pontiff also acceded to another request from Mulhouse. He guaranteed that anyone who fought and died on behalf of the Roman Church under the new Mulhouse banner was entitled to have his mortal sins forgiven on the point of death by the army chaplain.[163] The bull also wiped away any prior stains of ecclesiastical censure or excommunication that may have hovered over Mulhouse's fighters. In so doing, the pontiff made the banner a kind of spiritual shield – in other words, a way to insulate Swiss fighters from the moral consequences of their violence so long as they committed it in the pope's name. A similar cult of sacrifice for the banner – a form of civil religion, as we saw earlier – had characterized Swiss military ethics for centuries. Now it

---

[161] Mossmann, 1889: 474–7. [162] Dubois-Brinkmann and Delaine, 2016.
[163] Mossmann, 1889: 477–8.

came with papal blessing. The banner campaign that Schiner and Julius II undertook in 1512 addressed itself to the complex cultural framework of Swiss esteem. By funding gifts of embroidered silk to kindle both patriotism and loyalty, Julius harnessed the Cantons' self-regard as a tool of fealty. In an era of ongoing wars, the papacy managed with this simple gesture to court one of Europe's greatest weapons: the indomitable Swiss companies that had become the bane of most other armies. And with sumptuous papal banners, the Cantons celebrated their new found favor.

The papal gift was divided as soon as the Swiss received it. The Confederacy elected to keep the sword and hat in Zürich, and deposited them in the sacristy of their Minster. Although the rapier has survived in the Landesmuseum, roaches reportedly ate most of the bejeweled red silk and ermine hat before 1580.[164] The two consecrated pontifical banners – with the crossed keys of Saint Peter and Julius's own arms – also met an unhappy end. The Swiss Diet agreed to hang them in the Minster of the Abbey at Einsiedeln, where the Cantons kept other treasures, such as the throne of Duke Charles the Bold captured at Morat. They were most likely consumed in the cloister fire of 1577.[165] But the more than forty banners that Schiner gifted to the Cantons and cities have largely survived in various states of decay; some of them – as in Zürich, Basel, and Solothurn (Figures 13, 31, and 32) – are stunningly well preserved. Survival rates may have to do with the fact that several Cantons swiftly produced an identical but materially inferior copy, so that the reproduction could be used in battle while the original remained safe.[166] The fact that so many of the original flags inspired local pride, displayed in regional museums around the country, testifies to the success of this canny campaign to secure alliances through silk flags.

When banners and flags were presented as gifts, and equally when they were later recorded and remembered, the identity of the giver resonated through the textiles. The magnificent funeral celebrations of lords presented a propitious opportunity for collected, archived banners to be displayed as cogent materializations of alliance, favor, and triumph. Our consideration of obsequies reflects on both the lives and afterlives of these objects, as they found their way variously

---

[164] The report comes from Heinrich Bullinger's *Chronicle*: Durrer, 1907: 326–7, esp. 327n1.
[165] Durrer, 1907: 292.
[166] The receipts for Basel's copy date to 1513–14: Durrer, 1907: 286n1, 351–4. See also descriptions of originals and copies in Bruckner and Bruckner, 1942, Fahnenkatalog. Here we list only banners with "copies for use" (*Gebrauchskopien*), which are generally painted rather than embroidered. Appenzell: #19 (original), #20 (copy); Bern: #127 (original, with mention of copy fashioned by Niklaus Manuel in 1513); Fribourg: #270 (with mention of copy by 'Alexander der Maler'); Glarus: #340 (original), #342 (copy); Saanen: #584 (original), #585 (copy); Solothurn: #641, 642 (two originals), #643 (copy); Toggenburg: #729 (original), #730 (probable later copy); Willisau: #796 (original is lost, this is a slightly later copy); Zürich: #856 (original), #857 (copy).

into glorious armories and arsenals, mundane storage, or forgotten oblivion. At Francesco Gonzaga's funeral in 1519, around the catafalque were hung banners the lord had been granted by a who's who of Renaissance princes and powers: the Papacy, the Empire, France, Venice, and Milan. Under each of the standards, six men dressed head to toe in black brandished banners emblazoned with the arms of the potentates whose flags flew above. They were accompanied by the same number of men, dressed similarly in mourning clothes, carrying torches, and once again by six men bearing shields adorned with the specific emblems.[167] Here the visualization of the whole was greater than the sum of the individual parts. The dialogue between the flags manifested Gonzaga glory and masculine honor. They materialized the dynasty's networks of power.

Banners – some gifted, others captured, many passed down – punctuated all forms of courtly life. When the almost-seven-year-old Alfonso II of Aragon was invested as prince of Capua in October 1455, he was presented a newly blessed banner adorned with the arms of his grandfather, King Alfonso I. At an extravagant Neapolitan dinner the day prior, celebrating the boy's betrothal to the duke of Milan's daughter, a large sugar sculpture in the form of a fortress appeared on a golden platter. The Milanese ambassador marveled at the confectionary castle and informed his lord that it was "surrounded by many flags with painted vipers."[168] No doubt Francesco Sforza was pleased to hear that in far away Naples the Sforza *biscione* was seen flying over a castle, even a candied one.

Like armies, lords and courts were peripatetic in the fifteenth century. Even when banners did not accompany princes, they followed not far behind. In January 1473, Sforza Secondo sent a number of standards to his brother, Duke Galeazzo Maria Sforza, in Pavia. These included, among others, a crimson standard with the Papal keys, formerly in Milan's Duomo; a standard adorned with the arms of France, belonging to René of Anjou; one depicting Milan's patron Ambrose, with the inscription *Libertas*, perhaps dating to the period of the town's Ambrosian Republic immediately preceding Sforza rule; others decorated with seraphs or cheetahs accompanied by mottoes; and one presumably Venetian flag representing Saint Mark, or more likely his winged lion, with the phrase *Pax tibi Marce evangelista meus* (Peace unto you, Mark, my Evangelist). As we saw at Francesco Gonzaga's funeral, collections of banners constituted archives of affinity that served to amplify lordly majesty through affiliation and history.[169]

Renaissance banners at rest were tallied in inventories. The posthumous inventory of Sigismondo Malatesta, the lord of Rimini infamously condemned to hell by Pope Pius II, reveals through radiant silk and gold stitchwork the

---

[167] Malacarne, 2012: 2: 28.   [168] Senatore, 1977: 278.   [169] Simonetta, 1962: 7.

prince's more auspicious alliances, including with one of Pius's predecessors. We find a taffeta standard embroidered with the arms of Pope Eugenius IV, another of crimson taffeta, and two white sendal flags adorned with Este arms.[170] Valuable evidence likewise appears across generations in the inventories of Mantua's Gonzaga dynasty. The myriad banners registered in 1407, for instance, include one hanging from a lance bearing both an image of Saint George and the arms of the Gonzaga, adorned with crimson silk fringe; a silk standard emblazoned with a turtledove insignia; a scarlet silk *bandera* with Saint Mark figured in gold and probably Venetian; and three additional sendal banners, two marked with a black eagle and the third with unspecified Gonzaga heraldry.[171] Piece by piece, Renaissance lords stitched together authority through these precious textiles.

An inventory taken in January 1542, eighteen months after Federico Gonzaga's death, attests to the multitude of banners commissioned by and presented to Gonzaga lords throughout the prior century or so. These objects comprise a wide array of forms and materials, and their significance – and that of the political and military networks that they manifested – is revealed by the diligence taken to preserve the banners for many years and to register the circumstances of their incorporation into the Gonzaga arsenal, whether as gifts proclaiming service and alliance or as booty confirming conquest and triumph. Among the latter were a dozen "bandiere" of various shapes – and with diverse insignia – seized by Federico Gonzaga from Venetian and French forces in the early 1520s, in addition to three "old and worn" *bandiere* of French light horsemen still attached to their staves.[172]

Many of the most opulent banners were diplomatic gifts. Those offered to Ludovico Gonzaga, lord from 1433–78, and still in the dynasty's collections in the 1540s, include a sendal "standardo grande" from the Signoria of Bologna and depicting in gold Saint Petronius and the town's emblems, and a similar one bearing the devices of the dukes of Milan awarded by Francesco Sforza, who died in 1466. Extant among those given to Ludovico's son Federico (the grandfather of the Federico mentioned above) are two large sendal standards with gilded insignia of the Signoria of Florence, whom he served in 1479. The inventory's compiler asserts that another standard had been a present from Borso d'Este, from "the period in which he [Federico] was made Captain General of the league Ferrara constituted against the Venetians."[173] This banner marks Federico Gonzaga's military service not to Borso but to Ercole d'Este during the War of Ferrara – the so-called Guerra del Sale – of 1482–84. That

---

[170] Tabanelli, 1977: 400, 408. [171] Mann, 1938: 276–8. [172] Mann, 1938: 302, 306.
[173] Mann, 1938: 302.

Ercole's brother and predecessor Borso died over a decade before the conflict began suggests that memories embodied in symbolically eloquent and venerated material culture such as banners were not always precise, though they nevertheless echoed, even resounded. This instance, moreover, reminds us that if dynasties amassed and collected banners to furnish an archive of glory, the objects themselves were not always reliable narrators. Their profusion ensured that their keepers might lose track of whose glory was embedded in individual flags. Was it a gift from an ally, or a trophy stolen from an enemy? And in either case, who had it been? Such questions could become muddled relatively quickly – lost in a sea of silks – in these treasuries that constructed lordly power. These confusions, however, afforded opportunities for creative reidentifications, whether calculated or unintentional, that suited particular needs. As we argued in the Element's introduction, meanings imputed to banners could be as flexible or volatile as the textiles themselves.

Of course, standards in the Gonzaga armory had not only been given by foreign lords and civic governments. Many had been fabricated at home in Mantua, for the Gonzaga's own spectacles and armies. One radiant silk standard dated to the time of Ludovico, and thus could have been 70–100 years old when inventoried in 1542. Others decorated with Gonzaga *imprese* were associated with recent princes, Ludovico's grandson and great-grandson, including ten sendal banners of various shapes from Francesco Gonzaga's cavalry troops.[174] Similarly, the 1490 inventory of the Sforza ducal library at Pavia records a banner with the painted image of the long-since departed Francesco Sforza, an example of Renaissance portraiture that art historians have not yet begun to investigate. These portraits were singularly mobile and effectual, visible, as they must have been, to an array of audiences, some quite large.[175] Banners held in armories thus tell stories – sometimes jumbled, half-remembered, or misidentified ones – of victories, alliances, networks, and forebears. But even foggy recollections insisted that there was potential in these artifacts, since they materialized the deeds and privileges that elites relied upon for their prestige and glory.

6 Water

We have seen flags flying in the hands of banner-bearers, over the heads of armies, wrapped around bodies, and given as favors. They also rippled over fortresses and ships: the former always standing firm, the latter in constant motion. Castles and ships could even be combined: Roberto Valturio defined Byzantine *navi castellate* as "ships topped with castles" (Figure 35).[176] His 1472 treatise on warfare depicted

---

[174] Mann, 1938: 255, 302, 306, 314.   [175] Albertini Ottolenghi, 1991: 237.
[176] Valturio, 1483: fols. F4v-F5v.

The Fabric of War

Figure 35 Matteo de' Pasti, Between fortress and ship, in Roberto Valturio, De Re Militari (On the Military Arts), 1472. Woodcut. New York, Metropolitan Museum of Art, 26.71.4, fol. 192 v. Photo: The Metropolitan Museum of Art, New York.

two massive quinqueremes strapped together, the crenelated deck surmounted by a vertiginous tower capped with a crow's nest stacked with armed soldiers and pennons. Water made strongholds mobile; bulky maritime vessels transported war, trade, and dominion around the world. Fortress flags served as markers of sovereign geographies, and ships shared this salient feature as vessels for carrying mastery abroad: every reader already knows that flags became the preeminent tool that Europeans employed to stake claim upon lands and seas unknown to them. "Planting the flag" has become a universal act of possession. We saw Pisa's flag lowered and Florence's hoisted over Anghiari (Figure 28). Since then, people have erected them on mountaintops, ocean floors, and the moon.[177] In 1969, a triumphant image of US astronauts planting the flag on the lunar surface was so seductive that teams of NASA engineers toiled mightily to overcome the technical challenges of making a nylon flag seem to flutter in an alien atmosphere. Yet this dramatic, overdetermined gesture carried such significance that American statesmen assured allies and enemies alike that the space mission was not claiming possession or sovereignty. As President John F. Kennedy maintained years before the moon landing, astronauts would plant not a "hostile flag of conquest, but a banner of freedom and peace."[178]

We frame this section around water to illustrate how Europeans globalized their vexillary cultures across the waves. It also opens a wider vista, allowing us to investigate how societies around the world incorporated flags and similar objects in their own customs and in their engagement with Europeans. Traditions in Europe often mirrored, and may have been informed by, those of Asia and the Americas, yet we stay closely attuned to the material and social particularities that have made flags so central to global contests for dominance and resistance since the late middle ages.

While the flag-laden castles of medieval Europe loom large in our imagination – from fairy tales to Disneyland – it remains difficult to uncover when and how flags became regular fortress features in the post-classical world. One of the longest-serving citadels in Europe must be the Castel Sant'Angelo in Rome. Erected originally as the mausoleum of the ancient emperor Hadrian, in later centuries Roman magnates and then pontiffs harnessed its imposing mass as a stronghold. In 590, Pope Gregory the Great witnessed a vision of the archangel Michael atop its heights; sculptures representing Michael have surmounted the fortress since at least the fifteenth century.[179] But even more visible to Romans were the pope's standards, often immense in size. One undated sixteenth-century papal order requested

---

[177] Mohammed, 2002; Koch, 2022.   [178] Platoff, 1993: 1.   [179] Borgatti, 1890: 82.

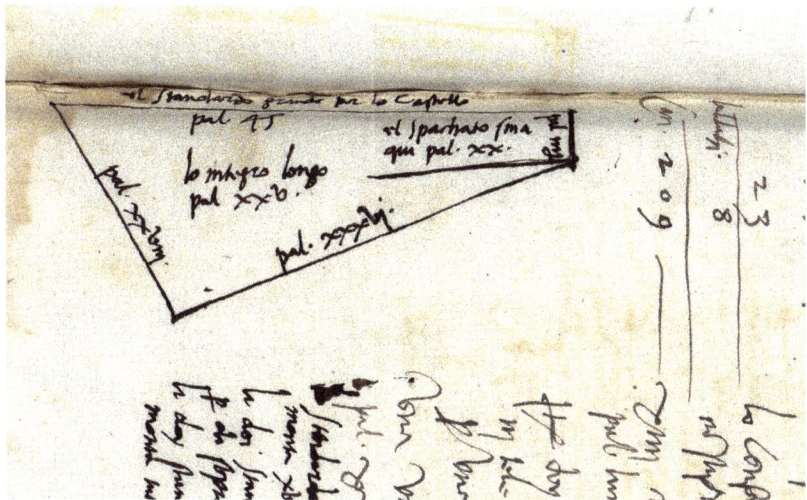

Figure 36 Drawing with measurements for the large standard at Castel Sant'Angelo, from a papal order for banners, sixteenth century. Vatican City, Biblioteca Apostolica Vaticana, MS Vat. Lat. 12343, fol. 104 r. Photo courtesy of the Biblioteca Apostolica Vaticana. All rights reserved.

the manufacture of sixty-five banners and pennons, five of them destined to fly atop the castle, the largest of which – mapped out in pen, with measurements included – was the "stendardo grande per lo Castello de Santo Angelo," a trapezium of taffeta measuring forty-five palms in length, long as a tennis court is wide, slit down the middle in a classic *gonfalone* swallow tail (Figure 36). Engravings of the castle from the sixteenth to the eighteenth centuries show this "large standard" as its most important feature, its towering flagpole held aloft with ship-like rigging and often bearing another angel on its summit (Figure 37). Castel Sant'Angelo regularly raised luxurious papal standards for celebrations and firework displays, but it also functioned as a military redoubt, the pope's refuge flying the red flag of war, for instance, during the sack of Rome in 1527.[180] High above Castel Sant'Angelo, the billowy standard was the papacy's most prominent projection of its sovereignty across the Roman sky, both in peace and in war.

Well before the global oceanic age, European maps of the world told a story about the place of flags in geopolitics. On the so-called *Tabula Peutingeriana* – a thirteenth-century copy of a fourth-century Roman wayfinding chart tracing major roads from France to South Asia – not a single flag flies above Eurasia's cities. Although the continents are dotted with settlements, the largest metropolises

---

[180] Gregorovius, 1869: 8: 544. We are unable to trace Gregorovius's source for these details.

Figure 37 Giovanni Battista Scultori, Castel Sant'Angelo, 1540–60. Engraving. London, British Museum, 1869,01612.369. Photo © The Trustees of the British Museum. All rights reserved.

(Rome, Constantinople, Antioch) are conceived not as castles, but as gigantic enthroned figures. How different the world looked a millennium later in Angelino Dulcert's 1338 portolan chart.[181] From Dulcert's Mallorcan vantage, the globe was awash in flags and each citadel – from Africa to Europe to Asia – flew an oversize banner announcing its ruling dynasty or its political affiliation. Was the "castle flag" unknown to the ancients who first traced the *Tabula Peutingeriana*? Could something have happened after 1300 to put flags on the map?

The notion that sovereignty could be conveniently shorthanded through flags may owe its elaboration to the professionalization of European heralds over the thirteenth and fourteenth centuries. These media wizards made exactly this kind of imagery their stock in trade, building an entire semiotic syntax that mapmakers borrowed. Contemporaneously, jurists like Bartolo da Sassoferrato worked to solder heraldic imagery to the legal order of European states. Maps were one of many media that communicated the latest developments of this vast experiment. Corroboration appears in other coeval sources. Dulcert's chart is echoed by the *Libro de conocimiento de todos los reinos* (*Book of Knowledge of All Kingdoms*, 1375–1400), a Castilian pseudo-travel book that survives in multiple manuscript copies. It visualizes each stop on its voyage through painted flags of the territories visited.[182] Even if the traveler of the *Libro* was imaginary, the banners – in many cases – connect to real heraldry, as far afield as the Timurid Empire, thousands of leagues to the east.[183] More than a catalogue, this manuscript visualized a vast Eurasian mobility, and did so through a parade of pennons.

Before following them across the seas, let us first consider flags as markers of possession. In Crusade chronicles, the imperative to seize enemy territory shows both Christians and Muslims raising their banners atop conquered strongholds, most contentiously the walls of Jerusalem. Once Frankish troops breached the city's Fatimid defenses in 1099, Fulcher of Chartres explained, they "straight-away raised the banner on top of the wall." That crusader flag rippling over the ramparts led the city's defenders to change "their boldness to swift flight."[184] Salah al-Din, the Ayyubid conqueror, raised his own flag atop Jerusalem when he captured the holy city in 1187. Recognizing the object's significance, a Christian soldier within the city "cut down the staff of Salah al-Din's banner from the heights of the tower and threw it into the mud," a show of defiance that "restored the citizen's confidence" to secure their walls.[185] Both chroniclers insisted upon the banner's power to inspire shifts in communal sentiment, since raising or dashing the flag visually announced triumph and resistance. Twelfth-century illustrated histories show banners atop fortresses less frequently than one might

---

[181] Paris, Bibliothèque nationale de France, Cartes et Plans, Rés. Ge B 696.
[182] Marino, 1997.   [183] Kadoi, 2010.   [184] Fulcher of Chartres, 1941: 68.
[185] Otto of Sankt Blasius, 1912: 42.

72 The Renaissance

expect. In Peter of Eboli's *Liber ad honorem Augusti* (1196), Palermo's skyline is more commonly topped with catapults and kite shields than with flags. Still, in one of its key episodes – Emperor Henry VI's assault on Salerno – a ladder-clambering soldier affixes the twin-tailed "imperiale vexillum" atop one of the city's towers, bringing it under Henry's sway (Figure 38).

Beyond popes, emperors, and crusaders, disputants of all sorts employed banners as territorial markers. Glimmers of this signification existed in

Figure 38 Soldiers of Emperor Henry VI planting the imperial vexillum on one of Salerno's towers, in Pietro da Eboli, Liber ad honorem Augusti, 1196. Bern, Burgerbibliothek, MS Cod. 120.II, fol. 132 r. Photo courtesy Bern, Burgerbibliothek.

antiquity. Roman commanders raised various signs over hillocks or fortresses to summon their troops and to signal Rome's supremacy.[186] One of the most eloquent links between flags and territory appears in the *Sachsenspiegel* (1220s), the record of long-standing customary law in the Holy Roman Empire. That text survives in several illuminated copies from the late thirteenth and fourteenth centuries, revealing how flags embodied and transmitted mastery from sovereign to vassal through the institution of the *Fahnlehne* or *vexillaria feuda*, literally a "flag-fief," a title granted directly from the emperor. Both text and image in the *Sachsenspiegel* convey how the flag manifested that privilege: "The Emperor bestows all religious princely fiefs with the scepter, all secular flag-fiefs with the flag" (Figure 39).[187] This practice in turn relied upon Merovingian investiture ceremonies involving a gift of the royal lance, one that began to bear a flag in the ninth century. The banner's import eventually overtook the spear's to represent the fief itself.[188]

In his juridical treatise on arms and heraldry, Bartolo da Sassoferrato acknowledged the legal standing insignia carried, and he reasoned that heraldry with the strongest signifying value was granted – and thus guaranteed – by a sovereign. Flags and shields, he explains in his opening remarks, served as the utilitarian objects on which these arms appeared, although he had nothing explicit to say about the role of flags in securing or bestowing land.[189] Still, Bartolo's interest in flags as

Figure 39 Eike von Repgow, Heidelberger Sachsenspiegel, early fourteenth century. Heidelberg, Universitätsbibliothek, Cod. Pal. germ. 164, fol. 21 r. Photo courtesy Universitätsbibliothek Heidelberg.

---

[186] Seston, 1980: 272.   [187] Eike von Repgow, 1993: 259.   [188] Bruckauf, 1907: 47.
[189] Bartolo da Sassoferrato, 1998: 27.

legal signs points to a long practical tradition of claiming territorial privileges through flags and legitimating mastery by flying or planting them, as outlined by Keller, Lissitzyn, and Mann in the 1930s, and by Patricia Seed in the 1990s.[190] A more precise genealogy of the legal origins of flag-planting and sovereignty remains to be written. Although we will return later to the cultural role of banners in territorial capture, this Element only opens lines of inquiry that require further study to lend this ubiquitous ritual a firmer grounding in law. It is worth noting the prevalence of flags as ensigns of state authority across Eurasia, from the Ottoman *sanjaks* (administrative districts, literally "banners") to the *hatamoto* ("banner guardians," or feudal lords) in Japan. The representational rhetoric for these legal ideas was well established in late medieval Europe. Italy's chronicle illustrators invented a now obvious-seeming visual language to depict moments when belligerents seized possession: The victor's flags fly upright, while those of the vanquished topple over or are tossed away. In the Lucchese Giovanni Sercambi's massive history, for example, Lucca's soldiers set their banner on the captured tower of Sangiuliano and hurl another to the ground.[191] In dozens of Sercambi's other illuminations, upside-down pennons signal defeat and loss of custody.

Sometimes these upturned insignias suffered humiliation through submersion in water. After enemy troops seized the Milanese duke's galleys in the Mantuan War of 1397, his ships' standards were sent to Venice, where citizens dragged them underwater through the city's canals to rebuke their Milanese foe. Sercambi's illumination shows Visconti's viper banners trailing through the lagunar waves.[192] Similar representations of naval subjugation recur in Giovanni Villani's chronicle (1341–48), such as his illustration of the Battle of Cape Orlando (1299), in which a ship bearing the Angevin lilies plunges the striped standard of Sicily's defeated king into the salty swells (Figure 40). This ritual is at the center of the enigmatic *Tavola Strozzi*, a *spalliera* panel depicting the city of Naples and its bay, where the Aragonese fleet returns after crushing the Angevin pretender's armada at the Battle of Ischia in July 1465 (Figure 41).[193] Sixteen Aragonese galleys fly King Ferrante's standard and those of his supporters. The victorious Aragonese flotilla in turn tows seven other empty ships with their oars lifted: boats rounded up from Jean d'Anjou's squadron. Six victorious galleys, as the Milanese ambassador reported in 1465, "pulled behind them the ships they acquired from their enemies with the banners low, dragging in the water."[194] The *Tavola Strozzi*'s main subject, in other words, is a triumphal entry with trophies on display, a humiliation of the House of Anjou performed at sea rather than on land. The

---

[190] Keller, Lissitzyn, and Mann, 1938; Seed, 1995. [191] Sercambi, 1892: 1: 393–4.
[192] Sercambi, 1892: 2: 38–9; Rihouet, 2021: 617. [193] Spinazzola, 1910: 127.
[194] del Treppo, 1994: 492n30.

Figure 40 Giovanni Villani, Nuova Cronica, 1341–48. Vatican City, Biblioteca Apostolica Vaticana, MS Chig.L.VIII.296, fol. 143 v. Photo courtesy of the Biblioteca Apostolica Vaticana. All rights reserved.

Figure 41 Florentine or Neapolitan artist (often attributed to Francesco Rosselli), Ships trailing flags in water, detail from the Tavola Strozzi, 1470-80s. Tempera on panel. Naples, Museo Nazionale di San Martino. Photo: Scala/Ministero per i Beni e le Attività culturali/Art Resource, NY.

practice had ancient precedents: Livy recounted the Carthaginian fleet dragging Roman freighters home by the stern as booty.[195]

Before triumphs could be celebrated, conflicts at sea required banners as military tools, often more urgently than on dry earth because the distance between vessels made communication so difficult. The Byzantine navy used what experts have called a "wardrobe" of flags, possibly up to 50 per warship, to signal each other using a rich lexicon of color and form.[196] Flag tactics remained a chief concern to Mediterranean fleets over the following centuries. The naval code of King Pedro IV of Aragon (1354, one of the earliest to survive) begins by stipulating that a standard – or what is often called a "pavilion" in seafaring parlance, from the Latin *papilio*, or butterfly – should fly over what we now know as the flagship. The regulation furthermore insists that guardsmen must defend it with shields provided by the king himself.[197] In these same decades English flagships painted red or gold raised lanterns, banners, and streamers to convey orders to the fleet.[198] A standard atop the mast became customary, but most notable in these maritime provisions are the complex semaphoric practices with handheld flags. A fifteenth-century Venetian naval manual teaches that mariners should wave combinations of banners from port or starboard to indicate both the number and type of approaching enemy ships to their commanding vessel.[199] Although raising the pavilion was usually a requirement (punishable by fines according to Venetian statute), some ships in open waters sailed incognito for reasons of discretion or self-protection, even though this sometimes resulted in friendly ships attacking one another.[200] Among compatriots, obeisance to warships flying royal pavilions could be made by sailing leeward and lowering inferior flags, as described by a French naval expert in the 1650s.[201]

This same author reasoned that the Muslim conquest of Iberia had transformed European flag culture. Before that time, he claimed, Europeans had only flown Roman-style standards from a transverse bar. After the eighth-century arrival of the Umayyads, flying their flags "sideways" from spears, the practice supposedly spread.[202] While the tale is unlikely, it does point toward resonances between European and Near Eastern traditions that likely share ancient Eurasian commonalities. Although those traditions were mutually intelligible in later centuries, they followed distinct cultural and religious logics. Consider the legend about the royal banners of the Sasanian emperors who ruled Persia until the rise of Islam in the seventh century. In his *Shahnameh* (*Epic of the Kings*, 1010), Persia's greatest poet Ferdowsi relates how the blacksmith Kava resisted the usurper Zahhak by tying his leather apron to a spear and using it to

---

[195] Livy, 2021: 416–17. [196] Pryor and Jeffreys, 2006: 396–9. [197] Capmany, 1787: 1–2.
[198] Runyan, 2003: 55, 64. [199] Mocenigo, 1420: fols. 241v–242v.
[200] Gluzman, 2020: 300–301. [201] Cleirac, 1660: 75. [202] Cleirac, 1660: 70–1.

rally followers against the despot. The virtuous King Faridun received Kava and decorated the apron with brocade, jewels, and silk, turning Kava's standard into "a sun amid the gloom of night" that "cheered all hearts."[203] Kava led Faridun's army against Zahhak, hoisting the enriched apron that became Iran's royal banner (*derafš-e kavian*), which reputedly grew to an immense size through the subsequent embellishments of each ruler.[204] The fourteenth-century Tunisian historian Ibn Khaldûn believed that these lavish trappings of Persian kingship were eventually absorbed into the self-representation of later Islamic kings, who had previously "despised pomp" but came to appreciate how banners broadcasted domination. Ibn Kaldûn called flags "the insignia of war since the creation of the world," and surmised that "this was also the case in the time of the Prophet and that of the caliphs who succeeded him."[205]

Just as Christ signaled triumph over death with his *labarum*, so also Muhammad raised victorious standards during his campaigns against pagans in the seventh century. Fabric fastened to spears recurred as a regular motif in these narratives. Muhammad's ancestor Qusay bin Kilab (400–480) ceremoniously knotted a white cloth (*liwa'*) to a spear before sending his chiefs to war.[206] In later generations, one of Muhammad's early converts unwrapped his own turban, tied it to his lance, and dedicated it to the Prophet's service, a gesture that consecrated what was already a widespread battle practice in medieval Arabia.[207] Muhammad himself putatively also bore a black banner (*raya*) and a standard named the Eagle (*al-'Uqab*), which an early hadith characterized as "black and square, being made of a woolen rug."[208] The early Hanafi jurist Al-Sarakhsi (d. 1090) wrote that *raya* referred to a military signaling flag while *liwa'* distinguished authoritative personages, but other scholars differed in their interpretations.[209] Still, the prestige of Muhammad's banner was paramount: At the Battle of Mu'tah (629), three successive commanders died bearing it before a fourth rescued it and mustered a withdrawal.[210]

In later centuries, the Prophet's standards were imagined in manuscripts, such as a late-sixteenth-century Ottoman miniature from the *Siyer-i Nebi* (*Life of the Prophet*, 1338) that depicts Muhammad's elderly uncle Hamza Ibn 'Abd al-Muttalib leading an army against Mecca's polytheists (Figure 42). The white furled object carried behind him has sometimes been identified as Muhammad's banner, inscribed with fragments of *surat al-saff*, or the "battle chapter" of the Qur'an, and with the *shahada*, the Islamic profession of faith.[211] In another leaf from the same manuscript, Muhammad is followed by three banners, two dark

---

[203] Ferdowsi, 1905: 1: 157, v. 47–8. [204] Ferdowsi, 1905: 1: 160, v. 51; Sarre, 1903: 358–9.
[205] Ibn Khaldûn, 1969 [2005]: 215. [206] Caussin de Perceval, 1847: 1: 237–8.
[207] Penzer, 1936: 248; 'Athamina, 1989: 324. [208] Alexander, 2010: 222. [209] Kruse, 1971.
[210] Tabarī, 1987: 152–60. [211] Rogers, 2002: 137; Shalem, 2000: 219.

Figure 42 Ottoman artist, 'Ubayd ibn Harith and Hamza ibn 'Abd al-Muttalib, the Prophet's elderly uncle, advance at the head of a force against Abu Jahl, in Erzurumlu Mustafa Darir, Siyer-i Nebi (1388), 1594–95. London, Khalili Collection, MSS 152.2. Photo courtesy Khalili Collection.

and one light, all similarly wrapped.[212] These too appear to represent the Prophet's standards, protected within rich coverings and bearing inscriptions. In another sixteenth-century illumination, the banner carried by a descendant of Muhammad is marked with the names of the Prophet, the four caliphs, and the Prophet's grandsons, and includes the *tawhid* (unity) formula, testifying to God's oneness.[213] Images like these reveal the totemic power of carrying even furled banners into battle, and their often lengthy inscriptions reiterate the apotropaic potency of text in Islamic cultural registers.

Textiles identified with Muhammad's standards had their own afterlives. When the Ottoman Sultan Selim I (r. 1512–20) occupied Mamluk Cairo in 1517, he was acclaimed inheritor of the caliphate and came to possess a flag identified as the Prophet's.[214] The Ottomans called it the "illustrious banner" (*sanjak-i sherif*).[215] Selim deposited it in the Great Mosque of Damascus for the annual pilgrimage to Mecca until Murad III moved it to Istanbul's Topkapı Palace in 1595.[216] A French visitor to the Harem in the 1670s espied the *Bajarac* (as he called it) in the sultan's bedchamber and marveled at its role in sustaining Ottoman authority: The sultan could quell sedition by displaying the banner, demanding the faithful to obey it, and condemning resisters as infidels worthy of death. By that time, Muhammad's standard had reportedly been sewn inside another textile: the flag of the seventh-century ruler 'Umar (r. 632–34), the second caliph. 'Umar's was in turn shrouded in forty layers of taffeta and then rolled in cloth dyed green, the color of the Prophet.[217] Other accounts describe cutting the banner into fragments to use as the basis for three new flags, each presumably acting as a substitute – and as vibrant reliquary containers – for the original.[218] Like many of the European flags we have already seen, this multiplication of copies efficiently pluralized and activated its holy power. The Ottoman banner that now hangs in Augsburg Cathedral, first documented in 1689, is probably one such replica. It was likely understood by the Turks – and possibly by the Christians who hung it as a trophy of war – as the Prophet's banner itself. A similar dynamic, albeit inverted, clung to the Ottoman banners captured by the Polish king in 1683, objects of middling importance to the Turks but construed by the Christians as booty of the highest value.[219]

Ottoman flags also frequently bore a distinctive feature inherited from the medieval Mongolian military tradition, the *tug* or *tuq*, a tassel fashioned from yak- or horsehair mounted atop a staff, sometimes as the finial of the flagstaff.

---

[212] Denny, 1974: 70.   [213] Yıldız, 2017: 67.
[214] On the implications of the Egyptian conquest for the idea of the caliphate: Casale, 2015.
[215] Ohsson, 1787: 1: 261–5.   [216] Zygulski, 1992: 19.
[217] Tavernier, 1680: 271–3; Ohsson, 1787: 1: 263.
[218] Zygulski, 1992: 20; Ohsson, 1787: 1: 263.   [219] Shalem, 2000: 219–20; Karl, 2014.

Tugs likely emerged from Mongol shamanism, which imagined them as anthropomorphic avatars whose hairy heads and lean bodies hosted mighty spirits. More than one version of the medieval black tug (for war) and the white tug (for peace) have survived in Mongolia. A rural monastery 560 kilometers east of Ulaanbaatar still houses standards associated with Genghis Khan (d. 1227), which the monks worship as his protective ancestor spirit.[220] In a Persian illumination of Rashīd al-Dīn's *Compendium of Chronicles* (*Jami' al-tawarikh*, 1306–11, illuminated 1430–34), the raising of six tugs dignifies the enthronement of Genghis Khan in 1206 as great ruler of the Mongols.[221]

For their numinous potency, tugs often topped flagpoles in the military cultures of the Mongols' successors (including Ottomans, Safavids, and Mughals) intermixing Muslim, Mongol, and Persian traditions. Babur (r. 1504–26), the founder of the Mughal dynasty in South Asia, appears in his illustrated memoirs, the *Baburnama* (1530, illuminated 1598) "acclaiming the standards in Mongol fashion" (Figure 43). Lengthy white ribbons of cloth wrap around three of the nine tall multicolored standards topped with tugs. A nearby deputy fastens a ribbon around a cow's shank. In Babur's narration, he and two allies stand atop the tails of the white streamers while the celebrant

> said something in Mongolian, and, facing at the standards, made a sign. The khan [of Tashkent] and all those standing by threw their koumiss [fermented mare's milk] toward the standards. All at once the clarions and drums were sounded, and the army standing in ranks let out whoops and shouts. Three times they did this. After that, the army got on their horses, shouted, and galloped around.[222]

Textiles acted as conductors of vital animal and human energies in this military ritual, elements of which still survive in Mongolian tug-worship practices invoking the ancestral protective spirit (*sülde*) of Ghengis Khan, in which the standard's staff represents the strength of the state.[223] The encounter between Central and West Asian banner cultures generated a material syncretism through the mediation of objects, in which each culture loaded cosmic, sovereign, and personal charisma into their standards.

Western European Christians knew many of these Islamic traditions, often from capturing standards in war. When the Catholic monarchs Fernando and Isabel conquered the last stronghold of the Muslim Nasrid Kingdom of Granada in 1492, standards visualized the transfer of dominion. Upon entering the Alhambra, agents of the Catholic crowns found seventeen Christian flags on display, including one that had been seized in battle 150 years earlier. Transfer of possession occurred in a ceremony in which the Christians raised a cross on the

---

[220] Zygulski, 1992: 69–99; Chiodo, 1997. [221] Rashīd al-Dīn, 1430–34: fol. 44v.
[222] Thackston, 1996: 1: 136. [223] Chiodo, 1999.

Figure 43 Mughal School, Babur and his army acclaiming the standards, in Baburnama, 1589. London, British Museum, 1948,1009,0.71. Photo © The Trustees of the British Museum. All rights reserved.

castle's highest tower and dipped the standards of Santiago and the Catholic monarchs three times before that cross. With trumpets, cannon-shot, and a declaration that Granada had been subdued, the Alhambra flew the flags of new sovereigns that day.[224] This was precisely the moment that Admiral Christopher

---

[224] Garrido Atienza, 1910: 314, 325.

Columbus invoked in the opening lines of his Atlantic voyage diary of 1492: "[B]y force of arms I saw the royal banners of Your Highnesses placed on the towers of Alfambra [sic]" and "I saw the moorish king exit the city gates and kiss the royal hands of Your Highnesses."[225] His letter to the crown from the same voyage recounted how thirty-three days after leaving the Iberian coast he spotted "innumerable people" inhabiting a huge number of islands "of which I took possession in the name of Your Highnesses with a declaration and with the royal standard of Your Highnesses unfurled; and there was no resistance."[226] With the horizons of Hispaniola before him, Columbus deployed the same techniques of seizure that Fernando and Isabel used at the Alhambra to subjugate long-desired lands.

Vasco Núñez de Balboa did something similar when he descended the mountains at Darién in 1513 as the first European to touch the Pacific shore. Balboa took a royal standard painted with an image of the Virgin and Child and the arms of Castile, and with the banner in one hand and an unsheathed sword in the other (a ritualistic pose adopted in Figure 11), he waded into the sea up to his knees before claiming the ocean for his sovereigns. He repeated this ritual again some days later "for further validation of the possession that [he] had claimed of these waters," in a canoe borrowed from a local chieftain.[227] Flags were crucial cargo in these early Iberian voyages. The ledgers for Magellan's 1519 fleet listed eighty banners shared across its five ships, not including the royal standard of painted taffeta. They cost slightly more than the price of bringing all Magellan's ships from Cádiz and San Lucar to Seville (25,000 *maravedís*).[228]

Contact between Europeans and Americans was in part negotiated through semaphores fashioned for peace and war. Chronicles informed by Indigenous Mexican witnesses picture banner-bearing Spaniards advancing on sea and land, as in the Dominican friar Diego Durán's *History of the Indies* (1579), in which European boats fly immense pavilions and the conquistador Hernán Cortés marches inland with a rippling crimson gonfalon.[229] When Cortés came ashore in 1519, he could not fathom that the Mexica or "Aztecs" he encountered at the capital of Tenochtitlan practiced one of the globe's most complex banner cultures. Flags of all shapes and sizes adorned the bodies of Mexica gods and humans alike; they were fashioned from materials including *amate* (bark paper), painted cotton, gold sheets, or the iridescent feathers of birds associated with divinities. Warriors carried hand-banners into battle, and representations of the war gods Huitzilopochtli and Painal depict them with small rectangular ones in their hands.[230] The Codex Telleriano-Remensis shows two warriors in the guise of

---

[225] Columbus, 1995a: 95. The editors believe the opening letter may be authored by the admiral's scriptorium rather than by him personally.
[226] Columbus, 1995b: 228. [227] Fernandez de Oviedo y Valdés, 1853: 3: 12–13, 15–16.
[228] *Relação*, 1519–21: fol. 3v. [229] Durán, 1579: fols. 202r, 204v. [230] Peñafiel, 1903: 21.

Figure 44 Codex Telleriano-Remensis, illustrated 1553–55, completed 1563. Paris, Bibliothèque nationale de France, MS Mex. 385, fol. 16 r. Photo © Bibliothèque nationale de France.

an eagle and a jaguar; a later Spanish annotation relates: "[T]hose who carried these arms of eagle and tiger were the most feared and valiant captains." To render this image even more legible to Spaniards, the reader has inscribed the word *vandera* (banner) inside the eagle's blank handheld pennon (Figure 44).[231] The Nahuatl root for such flags was *pamitl*; under the entries for *vandera* and *estandarte* in Molina's Nahuatl dictionary (1555), one finds "quachpanitl, quachpantli, quachpamitl," the prefix *quach* indicating a large cotton sheet.[232] But simple cotton flags only scratched the surface of the treasury of Aztec banners.

A fuller sense of their range appears in the Franciscan friar Bernardino de Sahagún's *Universal History*, in which he and seven Indigenous collaborators catalogued and illustrated numerous standards for captains and chieftains in a variety of materials. These included the two-poled *quetzalpanitl* (quetzal-feather flag), a *çaquanpanitl* (troupial-feather flag), and a *macuilpanitl* (five-staffed feather flag), among dozens more (Figure 45). The Nahuatl lexicon for

---

[231] The annotator was unaware that these warriors were dressed to be sacrificed: Keber, 1995: 177–8.
[232] Molina, 1555: 118, 240.

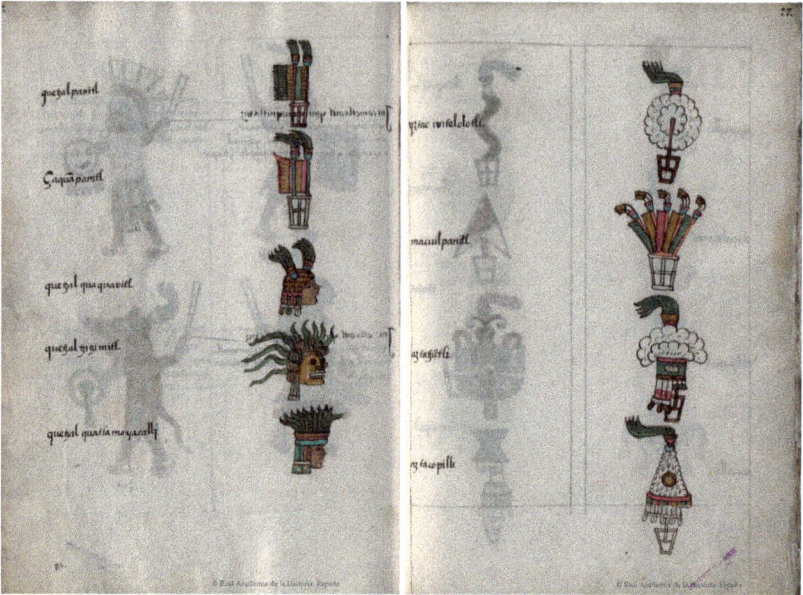

Figure 45 Bernardino de Sahagún and collaborators, Historia Universal de las cosas de la Nueva España, late sixteenth century. Madrid, Real Academia de la Historia, MS 9/5524, fols. 73 v and 77 r. Photo courtesy Madrid, Real Academia de la Historia.

military insignia is immense; Sahagún and his Nahua informants listed over ninety distinct words for warrior costumes, headdresses, banners, and shields.[233] Moreover, the work's illustrations indicate that flags were often attached to the body. Their grid-like staff bases allowed warriors to strap banners to their backs and display them above their heads. In his 1990 film, *Retorno a Aztlán* (*Return to Aztlán*) – the first full-length feature in Nahuatl, narrating the pre-Columbian dawn of the fifth sun in Mexica cosmology – director Juan Mora Catlett included warriors bedecked with colorful banners in this manner, inspired by manuscript illuminations.[234] In one such image in Durán's chronicle, we see Mexica warriors attacking the Spaniards' compound in the wake of Pedro de Alvarado's massacre of celebrants at the feast of Huitzilopochtli in June 1520 (what the Spanish called *La Noche Triste*). Four assailants wear banners on their backs, fastened around their waists and over their shoulders (Figure 46). One of Cortés's companions observed of these fighters:

> Each company has its standard-bearer (*alférez*) who raises the banner (*bandera*) on its staff in such a way that it is tied to his back, which does not at all

---

[233] Sahagún, 1550–90: fols. 68r-69r. [234] Lerner and Arnwine, 1992: 86–91.

Figure 46 Diego Durán, Historia de las Indias de Nueva España e islas de la tierra firme, 1579. Madrid, Biblioteca Nacional de España, MS Vitr. 26.11, fol. 213 v. Photo courtesy Biblioteca Nacional de España.

impede him in fighting or doing anything whenever he wants; and it is so well strapped to his body that unless it is torn to pieces, it cannot be untied or removed in any way.[235]

The pen-and-ink drawings in Glasgow's copy of Diego Muñoz Camargo's mid-sixteenth-century *History of Tlaxcala* reveal the astonishing dimensions of these warrior standards, some nearly equaling the size of the wearer's body.[236] Such physical coalescence with a military banner was familiar to Europeans who shared with the Mexica both a complex semiotics of martial organization and a commitment to fight to the death as materialized through binding ensigns tightly to the combatant's body.

Because warrior costumes and accessories often came as tribute to Tenochtitlan from the highlands or coastal regions, they embodied lordship over other territories and carried substantial exchange value.[237] This may also explain why the Mexica lord or *tlatoani* Moctezuma included such items when he sent noblemen with conciliatory gifts to the invading Spaniards. According to the Nahuatl recension of Book Twelve of Sahagún and collaborators' *Universal History*, these included "the golden banner, the banner of quetzal feathers, and the necklace of gilded pearls." The Spaniards, giddy from the sight of this golden

---

[235] El Conquistador Anónimo, 1858: 571.   [236] Camargo, 1558: fols. 276r-316r.
[237] Anawalt, 1992.

ensign, "laughed with joy, and like monkeys" began to "wave the golden banner and examine it as if it were speaking almost a strange unintelligible language."[238]

The centrality of feathered standards to Mexica military practice becomes clear in accounts of a decisive encounter between the Spanish and the warriors of Tenochtitlan at Otumba following the Spaniards' hasty retreat in the wake of the *Noche Triste* massacre. Squadrons of warriors confronted Cortés and his band, commanded by

> a leading warrior, richly dressed and plumed with a golden shield, and the banner with royal insignia that rose from his back was a net of gold that the Indians call *tlahuizmatlaxopilli*, which rose ten palms from his shoulders. The captain's name was Cihuacatzin, but he was called Matlaxopilli (taken from his commander's insignia) and innumerable men surrounded him, shining brightly and richly dressed.[239]

Several other chroniclers refer to this standard fashioned from a net of woven gold rimmed with feathers, confirming its name as *matlaxopili* or a variant like *tlahuizuntlazopilli*.[240] The term *matlaxopilli* is possibly a variation of *matlaxiquipilli*, or "bag-shaped net" which essentially describes the standard's appearance; the captain's real name was likely Cihuacoatl, the ruler's coadjutant.[241] This same standard – a gold-spangled net shaped like a droplet and crowned with a panache of feathers – adorns the shoulders of an Otomi fighter in the Codex Mendoza (Figure 47). Intended to display both his courage and his seizure of at least five or six war captives, it confirms Cihuacoatl's esteemed rank when facing the Spaniards. The fate of this standard and its wearer at Otumba in 1520 may show how despite their profound cultural differences Europeans and Americans shared symbolic and emotional economies regarding insignia of command. It may also, frankly, show a European reading of an event the Spaniards were only capable of construing by their own logics of victory and defeat. Such interpretive difficulties are inherent to these accounts. As they tell it, Cihuacoatl's ensigns of authority drew the Spaniards' aggressions, and he skirmished with Cortés before a soldier named Juan de Salamanca, riding a mare, impaled the Mexica captain with his lance. Salamanca "cut off his

---

[238] Sahagún, 1938: 4: 153 (book 12, chapter 12, from the Nahuatl version). The *Universal History* was commonly retitled *General History* in published versions through the twentieth century.

[239] Torquemada, 1975: 2: 228–9.

[240] Alva Ixtlilxochitl, 1892: 2: 401; Muñoz Camargo, 1892: 226. The *Gran Diccionario Náhuatl*, at https://gdn.iib.unam.mx lists an entry for *tlahuizmatlaxopilli* from Wimmer's 2004 dictionary: "sorte d'étandard que les Mexicains portaient à la guerre et qui consistait en un filet d'or fixé à l'extrémité d'une lance."

[241] Zantwijk, 2010: 31–2. Olko, 2014: 120, describes the *xopilli* as the "toe insignia," possibly for its resemblance to a bird claw. *Tlahuitzli* refers to a warrior's body suit or insignia of rank: Olko, 2014: 107.

The Fabric of War 87

Figure 47 Attributed to Francisco Gualpuyoguacal, illustrator, and Juan González, author, Codex Mendoza, early 1540s. Oxford, Bodleian Library, MS Arch. Selden. A. 1, fol. 64 r. Photo © Bodleian Libraries, University of Oxford.

head, took his banner, and speared others who were with him. This was so advantageous that soon the Indians, seeing the banner fall, stopped fighting and began to retreat and flee."[242] Salamanca offered the *matlaxiquipilli* to Cortés as a trophy "because he [Cortés] found him [Cihuacoatl] first and made him lower the flag and lose his spirit." Reportedly Charles V later bestowed a coat of arms featuring feathers upon Salamanca, an emblem his descendants used for generations.[243] By boxing these flamboyant feathers in a coat of Spanish arms, the Mexica banner was absorbed into the mechanics of European heraldry.

Cortés, however, did not keep the *matlaxiquipilli* as a personal prize; rather he ignited its semiotic agency in combat both for his own men and for the Nahuas. In Camargo's illustrations, Cortés himself wears the featherwork on his back as he spears a fallen warrior (Figure 48). The manuscript caption narrates how Cortés killed "captain Matlaxopile and took away the ensign he wore and put it on to encourage his people."[244] Later, the Spaniard presented the banner as

---

[242] Torquemada, 1975: 2: 229. [243] Diaz del Castillo, 1982: 1: 288.
[244] Camargo, 1558: fol. 264r.

Figure 48 Diego Muñoz Camargo, Historia de Tlaxcala, 1558. Glasgow, University of Glasgow Library, Sp. Coll. MS Hunter 242 (U.3.15), fol. 264 r. Photo courtesy of University of Glasgow Archives & Special Collections.

a gift to his ally, the Tlaxcala lord Maxixcatzin. Other Mexica loot – whether stripped from slain warriors, plundered from treasuries, or received as gifts – made its way to the courts of Europe, or was destroyed.[245] A folio from the

---

[245] Nowotny, 1947; Bleichmar, 2019: 1402–4.

Glasgow codex poignantly assembles Indigenous representatives of "the provinces and kingdoms that Hernán Cortés, Marquis del Valle, conquered," their Nahua emblems now interspersed with Catholic bishops' miters, their traditional insignia replaced by European cloth flags.[246]

Not long after Spain's conquest of Central America, news from the Asian side of the Pacific began to reach Mexico, followed eventually by visitors.[247] In the early seventeenth century, one such traveler was the Japanese emissary, Hasekura Tsunenaga (1571–1622), who reached Acapulco in 1614 as part of a Tokugawa mission to explore relations with the Spanish crown.[248] In Mexico City, Hasekura encountered a colonial metropolis awash in grey Franciscan banners, colorful feast-day processionals, and black royal standards.[249] In this era of relative peace, he would have seen few insignia of war, especially not in the Mexica style. But elements from both the European and Aztec traditions would have resonated with his own culture. Japan deployed a complex system of heraldry (紋, *mon*, meaning pattern or crest) whose logics resembled European practice.[250] As in Europe, banners could be personally altered by lords to celebrate valor: the daimyō Oda Nobunaga (1534–82) hand-painted on the white banners of the two Dōke brothers the phrase "bravest warrior of the realm" to mark their recent battle successes.[251] Samurais emblazoned their insignias across their heraldic and military paraphernalia, the most famous of which were published in a series of five scrolls known as *O-umajirushi* (*Great Standards*, 1639–44). The scrolls display the riotous variety of Japanese insignia, especially in shape: square flags (*shihō*), tall rectangles (*nobori*), streamered hoops (*fukinuki*), and back canopies (*horo*), the latter worn behind a combatant's shoulders and designed to inflate and protect its wearer from arrows as he rode. It, along with dorsal heraldic flags known as *sashimono*, were not dissimilar in conception to the Mexica *matlaxiquipilli*, both of them tools to heighten the warrior's frame and project his persona.[252] Still other standards took the shape of parasols, gourds, pompoms, trees, tassels, flower-blossoms, antlers, bells, helmets, and more. Indeed, the *mon* of Hasekura's master – the daimyō Date Masamune (1567–1636), ruler of Tōhoku, who funded the trans-oceanic expedition – appear in *O-umajirushi*: two layered umbrellas of black feathers topped with a golden panache, a messenger standard in the form of a helmet, a black *shihō* with

---

[246] Camargo, 1558: fol. 246r.
[247] For news from Japan in the early sixteenth century: Torquemada, 1975: 2: 426–7, 440–3, 565–71.
[248] Martínez Shaw, 2016; Knauth, 1972: 206–16; Luis, 2024: 189–92.
[249] Chimalpahin Quauhtlehuanitzin, 2006: 57, 83, 209.   [250] Hartmann, 2016.
[251] Gyūichi, 2011: 154.   [252] *O-umajirushi*, 2015: xvi–xvii.

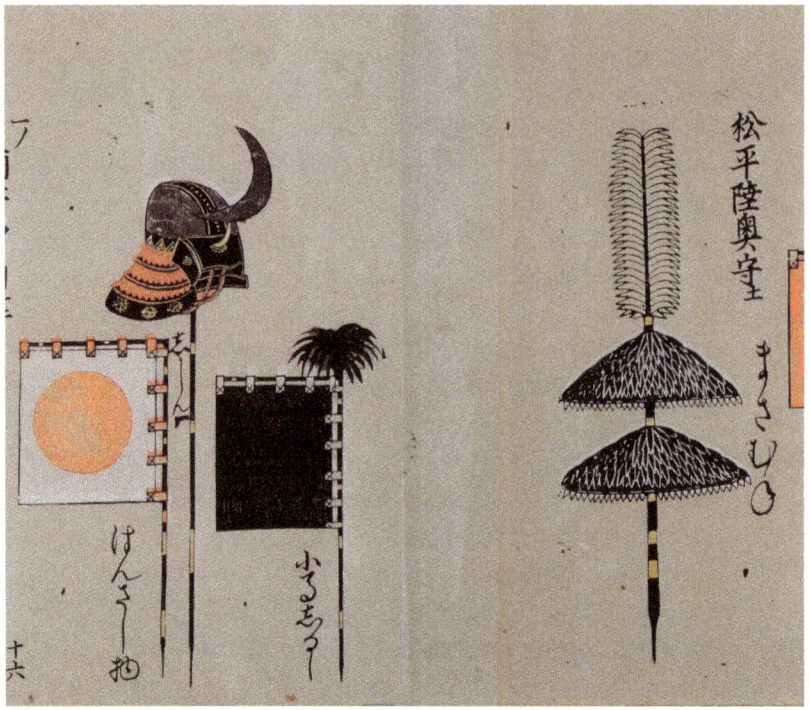

Figure 49 Heraldic standards of Date Masamune, in O-umajirushi, 1639–44, scroll 1. Tokyo, National Diet Library. Photo courtesy of the National Diet Library.

plumes, and a red disc rising on a white banner, the latter still familiar today as Japan's national emblem (Figure 49).[253]

Hasekura Tsunenaga continued his journey from Mexico over the Atlantic to the courts of Europe, where he visited sovereigns across the continent. In summer of 1615, while Hasekura traversed Spain, his lord Date Masamune joined the Tokugawa siege of Osaka to subdue the Toyotomi regime.[254] In a seventeenth-century painting of that battle, thousands of fighters charge toward Osaka castle: *fukinuki* rippling, *horo* inflated, and towering *nobori* bending in the wind as troops press forward – enough banners to make even the Swiss envious, a testament both to the vivacity and diversity of Japanese military display and to its tactical value, able to transform a chaotic battlefield into a legible chessboard, at least from overhead (Figure 50). While visiting the

---

[253] *O-umajirushi*, 2015: 19–20. Although depicted as white, the plumage in the standard is elsewhere described as golden: Turnbull, 1988 [2000]: 33.
[254] Pitelka, 2016: 128–42.

Figure 50 Battle of Osaka (detail), mid-seventeenth century. Osaka, Osaka Castle Museum. Photo in the public domain.

papal court, the Roman senate elected Hasekura as a citizen, and his *mon* – a Buddhist swastika crossed with arrows and topped with a European crown – adorns the top corner of the charter.[255] The same heraldic device floats on a curtain behind him in Claude Déruet's 1615 portrait of the samurai. Through the window behind him, we espy Hasekura's ship flying his *mon* atop the mast, a flag that rippled across two great oceans, a pavilion of diplomacy between Asia, America, and Europe.

Banners materialized powers and personhoods of stunning variety: imperial, institutional, regional, corporate, familial, civic, local, and individual, long before these objects came to emblematize nation-states. Today's national flags are the inheritors of these deep histories. Even if their materiality is now standardized and their signification circumscribed, embers of the complex meaning banners carried centuries ago still glow in them. As this final section has revealed, several premodern global cultures fostered display through raised ensigns for communication, ritual, recognition, combat, inspiration, and protection. Diverse as those cultures were, anthropologists propose that they shared not only these uses but also an underlying human disposition to signal dominance over others, a form of social symbol that functioned across cultures.[256] As historians, we welcome the search for such principles while we also seek the

---

[255] Meriwether, 1898: 97–100. [256] Shanafelt, 2008.

contingent specificities of past societies. One such aspect that becomes clear throughout this study is the way that banners accumulated significance across time, sometimes touched successively by divinities, monarchs, heroes, or glorious events whose sparks inhered in the object. In this sense, flags were often overloaded with significance; they came to be imbued with a surfeit of charisma, a particularly vibrant "aura" in a Benjaminian sense. Yet we have also seen how such mystique could be multiplied and distributed through copies or, conversely, dissipated through forgetfulness or neglect. It remains notable that the flag claimed unusually tenacious hold over groups and individuals, and the startling commonality that most cultures shared was a willingness to die or to kill in its name or to protect it. This reality still inheres in the modern flag, which the US Code refers to as a "living thing."[257] This animated stuff exerted – and still exerts – a specific form of enchantment, able to kindle a turbulent emotional fusion of pride, devotion, and potential violence. And while we have seen women as banner-makers, -bearers, and -collectors, these objects remain stubbornly appealing to forms of martial masculinity preoccupied with glory, victory, and righteousness. We must remain attentive to, and wary of, the troubling aesthetics that enable banners to decorate and ratify violent acts carried out in the name of greater goods.

---

[257] Shanafelt, 2008: 15.

References

Manuscript Sources

Camargo, Diego Muñoz. (1558). *Historia de Tlaxcala*. Glasgow: University of Glasgow Library, Sp. Coll. MS Hunter 242 (U.3.15).

du Prier, Jean. (1500–20). *Le Songe du Pastourel*. Vienna: Österreichische Nationalbibliothek, Cod. 2556.

Durán, Diego. (1579). *Historia de las Indias de Nueva España e islas de la tierra firme*. Madrid: Biblioteca Nacional de España, MS Vitr. 26.11.

Durand, Guillaume. (1374). *Rationale divinorum officiorum*. Jean Golein, trans. Paris: Bibliothèque nationale de France, MS fr. 437.

Mocenigo, Piero. (1420, later copy). *Ordini et capituli antichi et bellissimi sopra l'Armare et dissarmare et nauigar delle Galere et Armati*. Vatican City: Biblioteca Apostolica Vaticana, MS Urb. Lat. 821 pt. A.

Rashīd al-Dīn. (1430–34). *Jami' al-tawarikh*. Paris: Bibliothèque nationale de France, MS supplément persan 1113.

Règlement pour les gens d'armes promulgué par Charles le Téméraire. (1473). Paris: Bibliothèque nationale de France, MS fr. 23963.

Relaçión del coste de la armada de las çinco naos que ban al descubrimiento de Maluc. (1519–21). Seville: Archivo General de las Indias, *Patronato* 34, R.10.

Sahagún, Bernardino de. (1550–90). *Historia Universal de las cosas de la Nueva España*. Madrid: Real Academia de Historia, Madrid, MS 9/5524.

Printed Sources

Albertini Ottolenghi, Maria Grazia. (1991). "La biblioteca dei Visconti e degli Sforza: Gli inventari del 1488 e del 1490." *Studi petrarcheschi* 8: 1–238.

Alcega, Juan de. (1580). *Libro de geometria, practica y traça*. Madrid: Guillermo Drouy.

Alexander, David. (2010). "The Black Flag of the 'Abbasids'." *Gladius* 20: 221–38.

Alva Ixtlilxochitl, Fernando de. (1892). "Historia Chichimeca." In Alfredo Chavero, ed. *Obras históricas de Don Fernando de Alva Ixtlilxochitl*, 2 vols. Mexico City: Oficina Tip. de la Secretaría de Fomento, 21–445.

Anawalt, Patricia Rieff. (1992). "Warrior Costumes: The Codex Mendoza and Other Aztec Pictorials." In Patricia Rieff Anawalt and Frances F. Berdan, eds. *The Codex Mendoza*, 4 vols. Berkeley: University of California Press, 1: 240–1.

Arnade, Peter. (1994). "Crowds, Banners, and the Marketplace: Symbols of Defiance and Defeat during the Ghent War of 1452–1453." *Journal of Medieval and Renaissance Studies* 43(3): 471–97.

'Athamina, Khalil. (1989). "The Black Banners and the Socio-Political Significance of Flags and Slogans in Medieval Islam." *Arabica* 36(3): 307–26.

Babuin, Andrea. (2001). "Standards and Insignia of Byzantium." *Byzantion* 71(1): 5–59.

Bambach, Carmen C. (1999). "The Purchases of Cartoon Paper for Leonardo's 'Battle of Anghiari' and Michelangelo's 'Battle of Cascina'." *I Tatti Studies in the Italian Renaissance* 8: 105–33.

Bambach, Carmen C. (2019). *Leonardo da Vinci Rediscovered*, 4 vols. New Haven: Yale University Press.

Banker, James R. (2014). *Piero della Francesca: Artist and Man*. Oxford: Oxford University Press.

Barone, Juliana. (2009). "Rubens and Leonardo on Motion: Figures, Inscriptions, and Texts." In Claire Farago, ed. *Re-Reading Leonardo: The Treatise on Painting across Europe, 1550–1900*. Aldershot: Ashgate, 441–72.

Barone, Juliana and Martin Kemp. (2019). "The *Head of a Soldier* in the Ashmolean Museum and the Size of Leonardo's *Battle of Anghiari*." In Julia Dellith, Nadja Horsch, and Daniela Roberts, eds. *Götterhimmel und Künstlerwerkstatt: Perspektiven auf die Kunst der italienischen Renaissance*. Leipzig: Leipziger Universitätsverlag, 67–82.

Barsanti, Roberta. (2019). "Copie e derivazioni della Battaglia d'Anghiari: Una questione aperta." In Roberta Barsanti, Gianluca Belli, Emanuela Ferretti, and Cecilia Frosinini, eds. *La Sala Grande di Palazzo Vecchio e la Battaglia di Anghiari di Leonardo da Vinci: Dalla configurazione architettonica all'apparato decorativo*. Florence: Olschki, 307–32.

Barsanti, Roberta, Gianluca Belli, Emanuela Ferretti, and Cecilia Frosinini, eds. (2019). *La Sala Grande di Palazzo Vecchio e la Battaglia di Anghiari di Leonardo da Vinci: Dalla configurazione architettonica all'apparato decorativo*. Florence: Olschki.

Bartolo da Sassoferrato. (1998). *De insigniis et armis*. Mario Cignoni, ed. Florence: Giampiero Pagnini.

Battioni, Gianluca, ed. (2008). *1475–1477*. Vol. X of *Carteggio degli oratori mantovani alla corte sforzesca (1450–1500)*. Rome: Ministero per i beni e le attività culturali.

Baxandall, Michael. (1988). *Painting and Experience in Fifteenth-Century Italy: A Primer in the Social History of Pictorial Style*, 2nd ed. Oxford: Oxford University Press.

Bernett, Hajo, Marcus Funck, and Helga Woggon. (1996). "Der olympische Fackellauf 1936 oder die Disharmonie der Völker." *Sozial- und Zeitgeschichte des Sports* 10(2): 15–34.

Bertolotti, Antonino. (1889). *Le arti minori alla corte di Mantova nei secoli XV, XVI e XVII.* Milan: Prato.

Bickel, August. (1992). *Zofingen von der Urzeit bis ins Mittelalter.* Aarau: Verlag Sauerländer.

Bleichmar, Daniela. (2019). "Painting the Aztec Past in Early Colonial Mexico: Translation and Knowledge Production in the Codex Mendoza." *Renaissance Quarterly* 72(4): 1362–415.

Borgatti, Mariano. (1890). *Castel Sant'Angelo in Roma, storia e descrizione.* Rome: Voghera Carlo.

Borgo, Francesca. (2017). *Battle and Representation in Cinquecento Art and Theory.* PhD dissertation. Cambridge, MA: Harvard University.

Borgo, Francesca. (2023). "Summoned by Bells: The Soundscape of Leonardo da Vinci's *Battle of Anghiari*." *Source* 42(3): 170–8.

Bracciolini, Poggio. (1715). *Poggii Historia Florentina nunc primum in lucem edita, notisque & autoris vita illustrata.* Giovanni Battista Recanati, ed. Venice: Hertz.

Bruckauf, Julius. (1907). *Fahnlehn und Fahnenbelehnung im alten deutschen Reiche.* Leipzig: Verlag von Quelle & Meyer.

Bruckner, Albert and Berty Bruckner. (1942). *Schweizer Fahnenbuch.* St. Gall: Zollikofer & Co. Verlag.

Bruni, Leonardo. (1926). *Rerum suo tempore gestarum commentarius [AA. 1378–1440].* Carmine di Pierro, ed. Bologna: Nicola Zanichelli.

Büchi, Albert. (1923). *Kardinal Matthäus Schiner als Staatsmann und Kirchenfürst. Ein Beitrag zur allgemeinen und schweizerischen Geschichte von der Wende des XV–XVI. Jahrhunderts.* Zürich: Kommissionsverlag Seldwyla.

Bury, Michael. (2000). "Documentary Evidence for the Materials and Handling of Banners, Principally in Umbria, in the Fifteenth and Early Sixteenth Centuries." In Caroline Villers, ed. *The Fabric of Images: European Paintings on Textile Supports in the Fourteenth and Fifteenth Centuries.* London: Archetype, 19–30.

Buss, Chiara, ed. (2009). *Silk Gold Crimson: Secrets and Technology at the Visconti and Sforza Courts.* Cinisello Balsamo: Silvana.

Campbell, Stephen J. (2025). *Leonardo da Vinci: An Untraceable Life.* Princeton: Princeton University Press.

Cantor, Norman F. (1991). *Inventing the Middle Ages.* New York: William Morrow.

Capmany, Antonio de. (1787). *Ordenanzas de las armadas navales de corona de Aragona, aprobadas por el Rey D. Pedro IV año de MCCCLIV.* Madrid: Imprenta Real.

Capponi, Neri. (1731). *Commentarij di cose seguite in Italia dal 1419 al 1456.* Ludovico Antonio Muratori, ed. Milan: Typografia Societas Palatinae in Regia Curia.

Casale, Giancarlo. (2015). "Tordesillas and the Ottoman Caliphate: Early Modern Frontiers and the Renaissance of an Ancient Islamic Institution." *Journal of Early Modern History* 19(6): 485–511.

Cassee, Elly, Kees Berserik, and Michael Hoyle. (1984). "The Iconography of the Resurrection: A Re-Examination of the Risen Christ Hovering above the Tomb." *Burlington Magazine* 126(970): 20–4.

Caussin de Perceval, Armand-Pierre. (1847). *Essai sur l'histoire des Arabes avant l'Islamisme*, 2 vols. Paris: Firmin-Didot.

Cavallaro, Anna. (1989). "Pittori di stendardi del Quattrocento romano: i 'possessi' papali." In Carla Guglielmi Faldi, Teresa Calvano, and Mauro Cristofani, eds. *Per Carla Guglielmi: Scritti di allievi*. Rome: Amici del Tasso, 34–42.

Cavallaro, Anna. (1992). *Antoniazzo Romano e gli Antoniazzeschi*. Udine: Campanotto.

Cecchi, Alessandro. (1996). "Niccolò Machiavelli o Marcello Virgilio Adriani? Sul programma e l'assetto compositivo delle 'Battaglie' di Leonardo e Michelangelo per la Sala del Maggior Consiglio in Palazzo Vecchio." *Prospettiva* 83–84: 102–15.

Cederlöf, Olle. (1959). "Leonardos 'Kampen om standaret': En ikonografisk undersökning." *Konsthistorisk tidskrift* 28(3–4): 73–98.

Cennini, Cennino. (2015). *Cennino Cennini's Il Libro dell'Arte*. Lara Broecke, ed. London: Archetype.

Cerretani, Bartolomeo. (1993). *Ricordi*. Giuliano Berti, ed. Florence: Olschki.

Champion, Pierre. (1976). *Procès de condamnation de Jeanne d'Arc*. Geneva: Slatkine Reprints.

Chimalpahin Quauhtlehuanitzin, Don Domingo de San Antón Muñón. (2006). *Annals of His Time*. James Lockhart, Susan Schroeder, and Doris Namala, eds. Stanford: Stanford University Press.

Chiodo, Elisabetta. (1997). "The Black Standard (*qara sülde*) of Činggis Qaγan in Baruun Xüree." *Ural-altaische Jahrbücher* 15: 250–4.

Chiodo, Elisabetta. (1999). "The White Standard (*čaγan tuγ sülde*) of the Čaqar Mongols of Üüsin Banner." *Ural-altaische Jahrbücher* 16: 232–44.

Cleirac, Estienne. (1660). *Explication des termes de marine employez par les edicts, ordonnances et reglements de l'admiravté*. Bordeaux: Jacques Mongiron.

Cohn, Jr., Samuel K. (2008). *Lust for Liberty: The Politics of Social Revolt in Medieval Europe, 1200–1425*. Cambridge, MA: Harvard University Press.

Cohn, Jr., Samuel K. (2021). *Popular Protest and Ideals of Democracy in Late Renaissance Italy*. Oxford: Oxford University Press.

Cole, Michael W. (2014). *Leonardo, Michelangelo, and the Art of the Figure*. New Haven: Yale University Press.

Columbus, Christopher. (1995a). "Diario del Primer Viaje (1492–93)." In Consuelo Varela and Juan Gil, eds. *Cristóbal Colón: Textos y documentos completos*. Madrid: Alianza Universidad, 95–218.

Columbus, Christopher. (1995b). "Carta a los Reyes anunciando el Descubrimiento." In Consuelo Varela and Juan Gil, eds. *Cristóbal Colón: Textos y documentos completos*. Madrid: Alianza Universidad, 227–35.

El Conquistador Anónimo. (1858). "Relación de algunas cosas de la Nueva España, y de la gran ciudad de Temestitán México." In Joaquín García Icazbalceta, ed. *Colección de documentos para la Historia de México*, 2 vols. Mexico City: Librería de J.M. Andrade, 1: 568–98.

Contamine, Philippe. (1972). *Guerre, état et société à la fin du moyen âge. Études sur les armées des rois de France, 1337–1494*. Paris: Mouton.

Contamine, Philippe. (1973). "L'oriflamme de Saint-Denis aux XIVe et XVe siècles. Étude de symbolique religieuse et royale." *Annales de l'Est* 25(43): 179–244.

Contamine, Philippe. (2007). "Remarques critiques sur les étendards de Jeanne d'Arc." *Francia* 34(1): 187–200.

Corazzini, Stefano. (2023). *Cerca trova. Leonardo da Vinci e "La battaglia di Anghiari." Storia della ricerca*. Florence: Nardini.

Coulston, Jonathan C. N. (1991). "The 'Draco' Standard." *Journal of Roman Military Equipment Studies* 2: 104–14.

Covini, Maria Nadia. (2012). *L'esercito del duca: Organizzazione militare e istituzioni al tempo degli Sforza (1450–1490)*. Milan: Unicopli.

Dalli Regoli, Gigetta. (2006). "Riflessioni intorno alla 'Battaglia di Anghiari': Una nota sui 'nichi' di Leonardo." In Carlo Pedretti, ed. *La mente di Leonardo: Al tempo della 'Battaglia di Anghiari.'* Florence: Giunti, 80–9.

de Diesbach, Max. (1893). "Drapeau de Pavie." *Fribourg artistique à travers les âges*: planche XV.

Dei, Benedetto. (1985). *La cronica dall'anno 1400 all'anno 1500*. Roberto Barducci, ed. Florence: Papafava.

del Treppo, Mario. (1994). "Le avventure storiografiche della Tavola Strozzi." In Paolo Macry and Angelo Massafra, eds. *Fra storia e storiografia. Scritti in onore di Pasquale Villani*. Bologna: Il Mulino, 483–515.

Denny, Walter B. (1974). "A Group of Silk Islamic Banners." *Textile Museum Journal* 13: 67–81.

Deuchler, Florens. (1963). *Die Burgunderbeute: Inventar der Beutestücke aus den Schlachten von Grandson, Murten und Nancy 1476/1477*. Bern: Verlag Stämpfli & C.ie.

Deuchler, Florens. (2015). *Beute und Triumph: Zum kulturgeschichtlichen Umfeld antiker und mittelalterlicher Kriegstrophäen*. Berlin: De Gruyter.

de Wit, Theo W. A. (2017). "Pro Patria Mori: Sacrificing Life in Service of the Political Community." In Joachim Duyndam, Anne-Marie Korte, and Marcel Poorthuis, eds. *Sacrifice in Modernity: Community, Ritual, Identity*. Leiden: Brill, 33–53.

Diaz del Castillo, Bernal. (1982). *Historia verdadera de la Conquista de la Nueva España*. Carmelo Saenz de Santa Maria, ed. 2 vols. Madrid: Instituto 'Gonzalo Fernández de Oviedo.'

Díez de Games, Gutierre. (1989). *El Victorial: Crónica de don Pero Niño*. Jorge Sanz, ed. Madrid: Ediciones Polifemo.

Dubois-Brinkmann, Isabelle and Joël Delaine. (2016). "Restauration de la bannière de Jules II du Musée historique de Mulhouse." *Annuaire Historique de Mulhouse* 27: 167–71.

Durrer, Robert. (1905). "Das Schwyzer Panner und sein Eckquartier." *Schweizer Archiv für Heraldik* 19: 121–7.

Durrer, Robert. (1907). "Die Geschenke Papst Julius II. an die Eidgenossen." *Wissen und Leben* 1: 193–9; 249–60; 285–93; 322–8; 347–55.

Durrer, Robert. (1959). "Das Wappen von Unterwalden." *Beiträge zur Geschichte Nidwaldens* 26: 9–43.

Eike von Repgow. (1993). *Sachsenspiegel: Die Wolfenbütteler Bilderhandschrift Cod. Guelf. 3.1 Aug. 2°*. Ruth Schmidt-Wiegand, ed. Berlin: Akademie Verlag.

Elgger, Carl von. (1873). *Kriegswesen und Kriegskunst der schweizerischen Eidgenossen im XIV., XV. und XVI. Jahrhundert*. Lucerne: Militärisches Verlagsbureau.

Erdmann, Carl. (1933–34). "Kaiserliche und päpstliche Fahnen im hohen Mittelalter." *Quellen und Forschungen aus italienischen Archiven und Bibliotheken* 25: 1–48.

Even, Yael. (1984). *Artistic Collaboration in Florentine Workshops: Quattrocento*. PhD dissertation. New York: Columbia University.

Fabretti, Ariodante. (1842). *Note e documenti raccolti e pubblicati da Ariodante Fabretti che servono ad illustrare le biografie dei capitani venturieri dell'Umbria*. Montepulciano: Angiolo Fumi.

Fehrenbach, Frank. (2007). "Much Ado about Nothing: Leonardo's *Fight for the Standard.*" In Philine Helas, ed. *Bild-Geschichte: Festschrift für Horst Bredekamp*. Berlin: Akademie Verlag, 397–412.

Ferdowsi. (1905). *The Sháhnáma of Firdausí*. Arthur George Warner and Edmond Warner, trans. 2 vols. London: Routledge, Trench, Trübner.

Fernandez de Oviedo y Valdés, Gonzalo. (1853). *Historia general y natural de las Indias*, 3 vols. Madrid: Imprenta de la Real Academia de la Historia.

Ferretti, Emanuela. (2019). "Fra storiografia e mitografia. Amplificazioni, echi e distorsioni nella ricerca della Battaglia di Anghiari di Leonardo (1568–1968)." In Roberta Barsanti, Gianluca Belli, Emanuela Ferretti, and Cecilia Frosinini, eds. *La Sala Grande di Palazzo Vecchio e la Battaglia di Anghiari di Leonardo da Vinci: Dalla configurazione architettonica all'apparato decorativo*. Florence: Olschki, 3–27.

Fink, Karl August. (1947). "Carl Erdmann." *Zeitschrift der Savigny-Stiftung für Rechtsgeschichte – Kanonistische Abteilung* 34(1): 355–7.

Flamini, Francesco. (1891). *La lirica toscana del Rinascimento anteriore ai tempi del Magnifico*. Pisa: T. Nistri.

Formisano, Marco. (2003). *L'arte della guerra romana*. Milan: Rizzoli.

Franklin, David. (1995). "A Gonfalone Banner by Giorgio Vasari Reassembled." *Burlington Magazine* 137(1112): 747–50.

Frapiccini, David. (2013). *L'età aurea di Giulio II. Arti, cantieri e maestranze prima di Raffaello*. Rome: Gangemi.

Frazier, Alison Knowles. (2005). *Possible Lives: Authors and Saints in Renaissance Italy*. New York: Columbia University Press.

Fulcher of Chartres. (1941). *Chronicle of the First Crusade*. Martha Evelyn McGinty, trans. Philadelphia: University of Pennsylvania Press.

Garrido Atienza, Miguel. (1910). *Las capitulaciones para la entrega de Granada*. Granada: Tip. Lit. Paulino Ventura Traveset.

Gessler, Eduard Achilles. (1929). "Über die eidgenössischen Kriegsfahnen und das Glarner Fahnenbuch." *Zeitschrift für Schweizerische Geschichte* 9: 76–81.

Gingins la Sarra, Frédéric de, ed. (1858). *Dépêches des ambassadeurs milanais sur les campagnes de Charles-le-Hardi de 1474 à 1477*, 2 vols. Geneva: Joel Cherbuliez.

Gluzman, Renard. (2020). "What Made a Ship Venetian? (Thirteenth to Sixteenth Centuries)." In Georg Christ and Franz-Julius Morche, eds. *Cultures of Empire: Rethinking Venetian Rule, 1400–1700*. Leiden: Brill, 293–328.

Godefroy, Jean. (1712). *Lettres du roy Louis XII et du cardinal Georges d'Amboise*, 4 vols. Brussels: Foppens.

Goldammer, Kurt. (1956). "Die heilige Fahne. Zur Geschichte und Phänomenologie eines religiösen Ur-Objektes." *Tribus: Jahrbuch des Linden-Museums* 4–5 (1954–55): 13–55.

Gregorovius, Ferdinand. (1869). *Geschichte der Stadt Rom im Mittelalter*, 8 vols. Stuttgart: Cotta Verlag.

Groebner, Valentin. (2004). *Defaced: The Visual Culture of Violence in the Late Middle Ages*. Pamela Selwyn, trans. New York: Zone Books.

Gyūichi, Ōta. (2011). *The Chronicle of Lord Nobunaga*. Jurgis S. A. Elisonas and Jeroen P. Lamers, eds. and trans. Leiden: Brill.

Hahn, Cynthia. (2017). *The Reliquary Effect: Enshrining the Sacred Object*. London: Reaktion Books.

Hartmann, Julia. (2016). "The Japanese *mon* and the European coat of arms – a comparative study." *Arma e Trofeús: Revista de História, Heráldica, Genealogia e Arte* 18: 87–114.

Hatfield, Rab. (2007). *Finding Leonardo: The Case for Recovering the Battle of Anghiari*. Florence: The Florentine.

Hochstetler Meyer, Barbara. (1984). "Leonardo's *Battle of Anghiari*: Proposals for Some Sources and a Reflection." *Art Bulletin* 66(3): 367–81.

Huth, Otto. (1943). *Vesta. Untersuchungen zum indogermanischen Feuerkult*. Leipzig: Teubner.

Huyghebaert, Noel. (1963). "Iperius et la translation de la relique du Saint-Sang à Bruges." *Annales de la Société d'émulation de Bruges* 100: 110–87.

Ibn Khaldûn. (1969 [2005]). *The Muqaddimah: An Introduction to History*. Franz Rosenthal, trans. Princeton: Princeton University Press.

Joannides, Paul. (1988). "Leonardo da Vinci, Peter Paul Rubens, Pierre-Nolasque Bergeret and the 'Fight for the Standard'." *Achademia Leonardi Vinci* 1: 76–86.

Jones, Robert W. (2010). *Bloodied Banners: Martial Display on the Medieval Battlefield*. Woodbridge: Boydell.

Junginger, Horst. (2017). "Otto Huth." In Michael Fahlbusch, Ingo Haar, and Alexander Pinwinkler, eds. *Handbuch der völkischen Wissenschaft: Akteure, Netzwerke, Forschungsprogramme*, 2 vols. Berlin: De Gruyter-Oldenbourg, 1: 318–21.

Justinger, Conrad. (1871). *Die Berner-Chronik*. Gottlieb Studer, ed. Bern: Druck und Verlag von K.J. Wyss.

Kadoi, Yuka. (2010). "On the Timurid Flag." *Beiträge zur islamischen Kunst und Archäologie* 2: 143–62.

Kaiser, Jakob, ed. (1869). *Aus den Zeitraume von 1500 bis 1520*. Vol. III, part II of *Amtliche Sammlung der ältern eidgenössischen Abschiede*. Lucerne: Meyer'sche Buchdruckerei.

Kantorowicz, Ernst. (1951). "*Pro Patria Mori* in Medieval Political Thought." *American Historical Review* 56(3): 472–92.

Karl, Barbara. (2014). "Silk and Propaganda – Two Ottoman Silk Flags and the Relief of Vienna, 1683." *Textile History* 45(2): 192–215.

Keber, Eloise Quiñones. (1995). *Codex Telleriano-Remensis: Ritual, Divination, and History in a Pictorial Aztec Manuscript*. Austin: University of Texas Press.

Keller, Arthur S., Oliver J. Lissitzyn, and Frederick J. Mann. (1938). *Creation of Rights of Sovereignty through Symbolic Acts, 1400–1800*. New York: Columbia University Press.

Knauth, Lothar. (1972). *Confrontación Transpacífica: El Japón y el Nuevo Mundo Hispánico, 1542–1639*. Mexico City: Universidad Nacional Autónoma de México.

Knezevic, Igor. (2014). "The Green Banner of La Feria: Popular Revolt and Municipal Politics in Early Sixteenth-Century Seville." In Jan Dumolyn, Jelle Haemers, Hipolito Rafael Oliva Herrer, and Vincent Challet, eds. *The Voices of the People in Late Medieval Europe: Communication and Popular Politics*. Turnhout: Brepols, 167–84.

Koch, Natalie. (2022). "Planting Flags in Water." *Dialogues in Human Geography* 12(2): 302–6.

Kruse, Hans. (1971). "Rāya and Liwāʿ in Islamic Tradition." In Denis Sinor, ed. *Proceedings of the Twenty-Seventh International Congress of Orientalists*. Wiesbaden: Otto Harrassowitz, 283–4.

Laborde, Léon Comte de. (1849). *Les ducs de Bourgogne. Études sur les lettres, les arts et l'industrie pendant le XVe siècle*, Vol. I. Paris: Plon Frères Éditeurs.

La Marche, Olivier de. (1888). *Mémoires*. Henri Beaune and Jules d'Arbaumont, eds. 4 vols. Paris: Librairie Renouard.

Lambrechts, Pierre. (1945). "Otto Huth. *Vesta. Untersuchungen zum Indogermanischen Feuerkult*." *L'Antiquité Classique* 14(2): 412–14.

Léderrey, Ernest. (1962). "Les armées de Charles le Téméraire durant les guerres de Bourgogne." *Revue militaire suisse* 107: 368–82.

Lerner, Jesse and Clark Arnwine. (1992). "The Pre-cortesian Codices as 'Mexican' Film Language in *Retorno a Aztlán*." *The Spectator* 13(1): 86–91.

Livy. (2021). *History of Rome, Volume VIII: Books 28–30*. John C. Yardley, ed. and trans. Cambridge, MA: Harvard University Press.

Loomis, Laura Hibbard. (1954). "The Oriflamme of France and the War-Cry 'Monjoie' in the Twelfth Century." In Dorothy Miner, ed. *Studies in Art and Literature for Belle da Costa Greene*. Princeton: Princeton University Press, 67–82.

Lubkin, Gregory. (1994). *A Renaissance Court: Milan under Galeazzo Maria Sforza*. Berkeley: University of California Press.

Luis, Diego Javier. (2024). *The First Asians in the Americas: A Transpacific History*. Cambridge, MA: Harvard University Press.

Machiavelli, Niccolò. (1869). *Libro dell'arte della guerra*. Domenico Carbone, ed. Florence: G. Barbèra.

Mäder, Peter M. (1994). "Ein 'fast' zerfallenes Burgunderbanner: Untersuchungs-, Konservierungs- und Restaurierungsmöglichkeiten am Beispiel einer Fahne aus der Burgunderbeute." *Zeitschrift für schweizerische Archäologie und Kunstgeschichte* 51: 265–72.

Malacarne, Giancarlo. (2012). *Fruscianti vestimenti e scintillanti gioie: La moda a corte nell'età gonzaghesca*, 2 vols. Verona: Linea Quattro.

Manca, Joseph. (2000). *Cosmè Tura: The Life and Art of a Painter in Estense Ferrara*. Oxford: Oxford University Press.

Mann, James G. (1938). "The Lost Armoury of the Gonzagas." *Archaeological Journal* 95: 239–336.

Marino, Nancy F. (1997). "Introduction." In Nancy F. Marino, ed. *Libro del conoscimiento de todos los reinos*. Tempe: Arizona Center for Medieval and Renaissance Studies, xi–xvi.

Martin, Paul. (1939). *St. Galler Fahnenbuch*. St. Gall: Zollikofer.

Martínez Shaw, Carlos. (2016). "España y Japón en el siglo XVII: Las dos embajadas de la era Keichô (1596–1615)." *TEMPUS Revista en Historia General* 4: 72–90.

Masetti-Bencini, Ida. (1907). "La Battaglia d'Anghiari." *Rivista delle biblioteche e degli archivi* 18(7–8): 106–27.

McCall, Timothy. (2018). "Material Fictions of Luxury in Sforza Milan." In Catherine Kovesi, ed. *Luxury and the Ethics of Greed in Early Modern Italy*. Turnhout: Brepols, 239–76.

McCall, Timothy. (2022). *Brilliant Bodies: Fashioning Courtly Men in Early Renaissance Italy*. University Park: Penn State University Press.

McCall, Timothy. (2023). *Making the Renaissance Man: Masculinity in the Courts of Renaissance Italy*. London: Reaktion Books.

McGee, Timothy J. (1983). "'Alla Battaglia': Music and Ceremony in Fifteenth-Century Florence." *Journal of the American Musicological Society* 36(2): 287–302.

Mees, Bernard. (2008). *The Science of the Swastika*. New York: Central European University Press.

Melani, Margherita. (2012). *The Fascination of the Unfinished Work: The Battle of Anghiari by Leonardo da Vinci*. Poggio a Caiano: CB Edizioni.

Meriwether, Colyer. (1898). "A Sketch of the Life of Date Masamune and an Account of His Embassy to Rome." *Transactions of the Asiatic Society of Japan* 21: 3–105.

Meyer, Herbert. (1930). "Die rote Fahne. Begrüßansprache beim Göttinger Rechtshistorikertage zu Pfingsten 1929." *Zeitschrift der Savigny-Stiftung für Rechtsgeschichte – Germanische Abteilung* 50: 310–53.

Meyer, Werner. (1998). *"Der stier von Ure treib ein grob gesang*. Fahnen und andere Feldzeichen in der spätmittelalterlichen Eidgenossenschaft." In Alfred Haverkamp with Elisabeth Müller-Luckner, eds. *Information, Kommunikation und Selbstdarstellung in mittelalterlichen Gemeinden*. Munich: R. Oldenbourg Verlag, 201–35.

Moeder, Marcel. (1923). "Voyage à Rome en 1512 de Jean Oswaldt-Gamsharst, greffier-syndic de Mulhouse." *Revue d'Alsace* 70: 395–404, 452–61.

Mohammed, Patricia. (2002). "Taking Possession: Symbols of Empire and Nationhood." *Small Axe* 11: 31–58.

Molina, Alonso de. (1555). *Aqui comiença vn vocabulario enla lengua castellana y mexicana*. Mexico City: En casa de Juan Pablos.

Mossmann, Xavier, ed. (1889). *Cartulaire de Mulhouse*, Vol. IV. Strasbourg: Heitz & Mündel.

Motta, Emilio. (1899). "Il diamante del duca di Borgogna." *Bollettino storico della Svizzera italiana* 21(1–3): 33–4.

Muñoz Camargo, Diego. (1892). *Historia de Tlaxcala*. Alfredo Chavero, ed. Mexico City: Oficina Tip. de la Secretaría de Fomento.

Müntz, Eugène. (1882). *Les arts à la cour des papes pendant le XVe et le XVIe siècle: Troisième Partie (Sixte IV-Léon X, 1471–1521). Première Section*. Paris: Ernest Thorin.

Musci, Alfonso. (2011). "Giorgio Vasari: 'Cerca Trova'. La storia dietro il dipinto." *Rinascimento* 51: 237–68.

Nagel, Alexander and Christopher Wood. (2010). *Anachronic Renaissance*. New York: Zone Books.

Nelson, Sean. (2016). "Relics of Christian Victory: The Translation of Ottoman Spolia in Grand Ducal Tuscany." In Maurizio Arfaioli and Marta Caroscio, eds. *The Grand Ducal Medici and the Levant: Material Culture, Diplomacy, and Imagery in the Early Modern Mediterranean*. London: Harvey Miller, 75–84.

Neubecker, Ottfried. (1973). "Fahne (militärisch)." In *Reallexikon für deutsche Kunstgeschichte* 6, online at: www.rdklabor.de/wiki/Fahne_(militärisch).

Neubecker, Ottfried and Florens Deuchler. (1973). "Fahnenbuch." In *Reallexikon für deutsche Kunstgeschichte* 6, online at: www.rdklabor.de/wiki/Fahnenbuch.

Nowotny, Karl Anton. (1947). "Die Gastgeschenke des Motecuhçoma an Cortés." *Archiv für Völkerkunde* 2: 210–21.

Ohsson, Ignace Mouradja d'. (1787). *Tableau général de l'empire Othoman*, 2 vols. Paris: L'Imprimerie de Monsieur.

Olko, Justyna. (2014). *Insignia of Rank in the Nahua World: From the Fifteenth to the Seventeenth Century*. Boulder: University Press of Colorado.

Otto of Sankt Blasius. (1912). *Chronica*. Adolfus Hofmeister, ed. Hanover: Impensis Bibliopolii Hahniani.

O-umajirushi: A 17th-Century Compendium of Samurai Heraldry. (2015). Xavid "Kihō" Pretzer, trans. Cambridge, MA: The Academy of the Four Directions.

Pacheco, Francisco. (1649). *Arte de la pintura: su antiguedad y grandezas*. Seville: Simon Faxardo.

Pardi, Giuseppe, ed. (1923–33). *Diario ferrarese dall'anno 1409 sino al 1502*. Bologna: Zanichelli.

Pastoureau, Michel. (2004). *Une histoire symbolique du Moyen Âge occidental*. Paris: Seuil.

Pedretti, Carlo, ed. (2006a). *La mente di Leonardo: Al tempo della 'Battaglia di Anghiari.'* Florence: Giunti.

Pedretti, Carlo. (2006b). "Leonardo, 1505 e dopo." In Carlo Pedretti, ed. *La mente di Leonardo: Al tempo della 'Battaglia di Anghiari.'* Florence: Giunti, 23–32.

Pélissier, Léon G, ed. (1912). *Documents relatifs au règne de Louis XII et à sa politique en Italie*. Montpellier: Imprimerie Générale du Midi.

Peñafiel, Antonio. (1903). *Indumentaria antigua: Vestidos guerreros y civiles de los Mexicanos*. Mexico City: Oficina Tip. de la Secretaría de Fomento.

Penzer, Norman M. (1936). *The Harem*. Philadelphia: J.B. Lippincott.

Pitelka, Morgan. (2016). *Spectacular Accumulation: Material Culture, Tokugawa Ieyasu, and Samurai Sociability*. Honolulu: University of Hawai'i Press.

Platoff, Anne M. (1993). "*Where No Flag Has Gone Before: Political and Technical Aspects of Placing a Flag on the Moon*." Contractor Report 188251. Washington, DC: NASA.

Polcri, Franco. (2006). "La 'Battaglia di Anghiari' prima di Leonardo: Dai cassoni alla pittura murale." In Carlo Pedretti, ed. *La mente di Leonardo: Al tempo della 'Battaglia di Anghiari.'* Florence: Giunti, 72–9.

Porro Lambertenghi, Giulio. (1878). "Lettere di Galeazzo Maria Sforza." *Archivio storico lombardo* 5(1): 107–29.

Predonzani, Massimo. (2010). *Anghiari 29 giugno 1440. La battaglia, l'iconografia, le compagnie di ventura, l'araldica*. Rimini: Il Cerchio.

Pryor, John H. and Elizabeth M. Jeffreys. (2006). *The Age of the ΔΡΟΜΩΝ: The Byzantine Navy, ca. 500–1204*. Leiden: Brill.

Richardson, Jessica N. (2024). "Natural Calamities, Litany, and Banners: The Intercession of the Virgin and Christ in Fourteenth- and Fifteenth-Century Florence." *Mitteilungen des Kunsthistorischen Institutes in Florenz* 65(1): 44–71.

Rihouet, Pascale. (2019). *Art Moves: The Material Culture of Processions in Renaissance Perugia*. Turnhout: Harvey Miller.

Rihouet, Pascale. (2021). "Art, Ritual and Law in the Life of Heraldic Flags in Late Medieval and Renaissance Italy." In Anne Wagner and Sarah Marusek, eds. *Flags, Color, and the Legal Narrative: Public Memory, Identity, and Critique*. Berlin: Springer, 605–20.

Rogers, John M. (2002). *Empire of the Sultans: Ottoman Art from the Collection of Nasser D. Khalili*. London: Nour Foundation.

Rubinstein, Nicolai. (1991). "Machiavelli and the Mural Decoration of the Hall of the Great Council of Florence." In Ronald G. Kecks, ed. *Musagetes: Festschrift für Wolfram Prinz zu seinem 60. Geburtstag am 5. Februar 1989*. Berlin: Mann Verlag, 275–85.

Rubinstein, Nicolai. (1995). *The Palazzo Vecchio, 1298–1532: Government, Architecture and Imagery in the Civic Palace of the Florentine Republic*. Oxford: Oxford University Press.

Runyan, Timothy J. (2003). "Naval Power and Maritime Technology during the Hundred Years War." In John B. Hattendorf and Richard W. Unger, eds. *War at Sea in the Middle Ages and the Renaissance*. Woodbridge: Boydell, 53–67.

Sahagún, Bernardino de. (1938). *Historia general de las cosas de Nueva España*, 5 vols. Mexico City: Editorial Pedro Robredo.

Sarre, Friedrich. (1903). "Die altorientalischen Feldzeichen, mit besonderer Berücksichtigung eines unveröffentlichten Stückes." *Klio* 3: 333–71.

Schib, Karl. (1939). "Schaffhausens Anteil am Sempacherkrieg." *Schaffhauser Beiträge zur vaterländischen Geschichte* 16: 213–22.

Schramm, Percy Ernst. (1954–56). "Beiträge zur Geschichte der Fahnen und ihrer Verwandten." In *Herrschaftszeichen und Staatssymbolik. Beiträge zu ihrer Geschichte vom 3. bis zum 16. Jahrhundert*, 3 vols. Stuttgart: Anton Hiersemann, 2: 643–73.

Schreiner, Klaus. (2011). "Signa Victricia. Heilige Zeichen in kriegerischen Konflikten des Mittelalters." In *Rituale, Zeichen, Bilder. Formen und Funktionen symbolischer Kommunikation im Mittelalter*. Cologne: Böhlau Verlag, 13–63.

Schubring, Paul. (1912 and 1913). "Cassoni Panels in English Private Collections." *Burlington Magazine* 22(117): 158–65 and 22(118): 196–203.

Schwering, Max-Leo. (1974). "Historische Fahnen als ikonographisches und konservatorisches Problem." *Waffen- und Kostümkunde* 16: 65–74.

Seed, Patricia. (1995). *Ceremonies of Possession in Europe's Conquest of the New World, 1492–1640*. Cambridge: Cambridge University Press.

Senatore, Francesco, ed. (1977). *1444–2 luglio 1458*. Vol. I of *Dispacci sforzeschi da Napoli*. Salerno: Carlone.

Sercambi, Giovanni. (1892). *Le croniche*. Salvatore Bongi, ed. 2 vols. Lucca: Tipografia Giusti.

Seston, William. (1980). "Feldzeichen." In *Scripta varia: Mélanges d'histoire romaine, de droit, d'épigraphie et d'histoire du christianisme*. Rome: École française de Rome, 263–81.

Shalem, Avinoam. (2000). "The 'Banner of the Prophet' in the Cathedral of Augsburg." In Zeynep Yasa Yaman, ed. *Sanatta Etkileşim / Interactions in Art*. Ankara: Türkiye Bankası, 216–21.

Shanafelt, Robert. (2008). "The Nature of Flag Power: How Flags Entail Dominance, Subordination, and Social Solidarity." *Politics and the Life Sciences* 27(2): 13–27.

Simonetta, Cicco. (1962). *I diari di Cicco Simonetta*. Alfio Rosario Natale, ed. Milan: Giuffrè.

Six, Georges. (1905). *La Bataille de Mons-en-Pévèle, 18 août 1304*. Paris: Berger-Levrault et C.ie.

Spinazzola, Vittorio. (1910). "Di Napoli antica e della sua topografia in una tavola del XV secolo rappresentante il trionfo navale di Ferrante d'Aragona dopo la battaglia di Ischia." *Bollettino d'Arte* 4(4): 125–43.

Steinberg, Leo. (2001). *Leonardo's Incessant Last Supper*. New York: Zone Books.

Strohmaier, Patricia. (2017). "Vom liturgischen Textil zum Werbebanner? Zwei byzantinische Goldstickereien im Dom zu Halberstadt." *Zeitschrift für Kunstgeschichte* 80: 219–46.

Tabanelli, Mario. (1977). *Sigismondo Pandolfo Malatesta, signore del Medioevo e del Rinascimento*. Faenza: Fratelli Lega.

Tabarī. (1987). *The Foundation of the Community*. Vol. VII of *The History of al-Tabarī*. William Montgomery Watt and Michael V. McDonald, trans. Albany: State University of New York Press.

Tavernier, Jean-Baptiste. (1680). *Nouvelle relation de l'interieur du serrail du Grand Seigneur*. Paris: Gervais Clouzier.

Thackston, Wheeler M., ed. and trans. (1996). *The Baburnama: Memoirs of Babur, Prince and Emperor*, 2 vols. Oxford: Oxford University Press.

Toffanello, Marcello. (2010). *Le arti a Ferrara nel quattrocento: Gli artisti e la corte*. Ferrara: Edisai.

Torquemada, Juan de. (1975). *Monarquía Indiana*, 5 vols. Mexico City: UNAM Instituto de Investigaciones Históricas.

Trexler, Richard C. (1984). "Follow the Flag: The Ciompi Revolt Seen from the Streets." *Bibliothèque d'Humanisme et Renaissance* 46(2): 357–92.

Turnbull, Stephen. (1988 [2000]). *The Samurai Sourcebook*. London: Cassel.

Vallière, Paul de. (1908). "Histoire du drapeau Suisse." *Revue militaire suisse* 53: 529–623.

Valturio, Roberto. (1483). *Opera de facti e precepti militari di lo excellente misier Roberto Valtvrio ariminese*. Verona: Bonino Bonini.

Vasari, Giorgio. (1879). *Le vite de' più eccellenti pittori, scultori ed architettori*, Vol. IV. Gaetano Milanesi, ed. Florence: Sansoni.

Vevey, Bernard de. (1943). *Le livre des drapeaux de Fribourg (Fahnenbuch) de Pierre Crolot, 1648*. Fribourg: Société d'Histoire du Canton de Fribourg.

Virmani, Arundhati. (2008). *A National Flag for India: Rituals, Nationalism, and the Politics of Sentiment*. Ranikhet: Permanent Black.

Weber, Christoph Friedrich. (2006). "Eine eigene Sprache der Politik: Heraldische Symbolik in italienischen Stadtkommunen des Mittelalters." *Zeitschrift für Historische Forschung* 33(4): 523–64.

Weber, Christoph Friedrich. (2011). *Zeichen der Ordnung und des Aufruhrs. Heraldische Symbolik in italienischen Stadtkommunen des Mittelalters*. Cologne: Böhlau Verlag.

Wolfthal, Diane. (1985). "Agnes van den Bossche: Early Netherlandish Painter." *Woman's Art Journal* 6(1): 8–11.

Wolfthal, Diane. (1989). *The Beginnings of Netherlandish Canvas Painting, 1400–1530*. Cambridge: Cambridge University Press.

Yıldız, Özlem. (2017). *The Sultan and His Commanders: Representations of Ideal Leadership in the Şehnāme-i Nādirī*. MA thesis. Istanbul: Sabancı University.

Zantwijk, Rudolf van. (2010). "La política y la estrategia militar de Cuitlahuatzin." *Estudios de Cultura Náhuatl* 4: 19–39.

Zöllner, Frank. (1991). "Rubens Reworks Leonardo: The Fight for the Standard." *Achademia Leonardi Vinci* 4: 177–90.

Zug Tucci, Hannelore. (1985). "Il carroccio nella vita comunale italiana." *Quellen und Forschungen aus italienischen Archiven und Bibliotheken* 65: 1–104.

Żygulski, Zdzisław. (1992). *Ottoman Art in the Service of the Empire*. New York: New York University Press.

Acknowledgments

The authors thank Julia Horne for suggesting that our study of banners should be a book while Tim was visiting Sydney on a SSSHARC fellowship. We are grateful to Jonathan Nelson for his encouragement and feedback and to Sean Roberts for suggesting the title. The anonymous peer reviewers' sharp, thorough suggestions and criticisms challenged us and strengthened the text. We also thank Aiofe Brady, Caroline Campbell, Michael Depreter, Mark Erdmann, Leslie Geddes, Christiane Gruber, Lynne Hartnett, Shiqiu Liu, Louise Marshall, Susan Marti, Stuart McManus, Drisana Misra, James Morton, Scott Nethersole, Jill Pederson, Sophie Pitman, Sasha Rossman, Sarah Rosenthal, Natalie Ruppel, Pat Simons, Paul Steege, and Jakob Weber. We gratefully acknowledge audiences at the Sydney "Japan and the Indo-Pacific" workshop; AAANZ Melbourne; Chinese University of Hong Kong; the "Flag This!" conference at the University of Bern; and the Villanova History Department's faculty forum. A Villanova University Summer Grant and the Bernard Lucci Endowed Chair in Italian Studies provided funds for research and the publication of images.

The Renaissance

John Henderson
Birkbeck, University of London, and Wolfson College, University of Cambridge

John Henderson is Emeritus Professor of Italian Renaissance History at Birkbeck, University of London, and Emeritus Fellow of Wolfson College, University of Cambridge. His recent publications include *Florence Under Siege: Surviving Plague in an Early Modern City* (2019), and *Plague and the City*, edited with Lukas Engelmann and Christos Lynteris (2019), and *Representing Infirmity: Diseased Bodies in Renaissance Italy*, edited with Fredrika Jacobs and Jonathan K. Nelson (2021). He is also the author of *Piety and Charity in Late Medieval Florence* (1994); *The Great Pox: The French Disease in Renaissance Europe*, with Jon Arrizabalaga and Roger French (1997); and *The Renaissance Hospital: Healing the Body and Healing the Soul* (2006). Forthcoming publications include a Cambridge Element, *Representing and Experiencing the Great Pox in Renaissance Italy* (2023).

Jonathan K. Nelson
Syracuse University Florence

Jonathan K. Nelson teaches Italian Renaissance Art at Syracuse University Florence and is research associate at the Harvard Kennedy School. His books include *Filippino Lippi* (2004, with Patrizia Zambrano); *Leonardo e la reinvenzione della figura femminile* (2007), *The Patron's Payoff: Conspicuous Commissions in Italian Renaissance Art* (2008, with Richard J. Zeckhauser), *Filippino Lippi* (2022); and he co-edited *Representing Infirmity. Diseased Bodies in Renaissance Italy* (2021). He co-curated museum exhibitions dedicated to Michelangelo (2002), Botticelli and Filippino (2004), Robert Mapplethorpe (2009), and Marcello Guasti (2019), and two online exhibitions about Bernard Berenson (2012, 2015). Forthcoming publications include a Cambridge Element, *Risks in Renaissance Art: Production, Purchase, Reception* (2023).

Assistant Editor
Sarah McBryde, *Birkbeck, University of London*

Editorial Board
Wendy Heller, *Scheide Professor of Music History, Princeton University*
Giorgio Riello, *Chair of Early Modern Global History, European University Institute, Florence*
Ulinka Rublack, *Professor of Early Modern History, St Johns College, University of Cambridge*
Jane Tylus, *Andrew Downey Orrick Professor of Italian and Professor of Comparative Literature, Yale University*

About the Series
Timely, concise, and authoritative, Elements in the Renaissance showcases cutting-edge scholarship by both new and established academics. Designed to introduce students, researchers, and general readers to key questions in current research, the volumes take multi-disciplinary and transnational approaches to explore the conceptual, material, and cultural frameworks that structured Renaissance experience.

Cambridge Elements

The Renaissance

Elements in the Series

The World in Dress: Costume Books across Italy, Europe, and the East
Giulia Calvi

Cinderella's Glass Slipper: Towards a Cultural History of Renaissance Materialities
Genevieve Warwick

The Renaissance on the Road: Mobility, Migration and Cultural Exchange
Rosa Salzberg

Measuring in the Renaissance: An Introduction
Emanuele Lugli

Elite Women and the Italian Wars, 1494–1559
Susan Broomhall and Carolyn James

Risks in Renaissance Art: Production, Purchase, and Reception
Jonathan K. Nelson and Richard J. Zeckhauser

Senses of Space in the Early Modern World
Nicholas Terpstra

Plague, Towns and Monarchy in Early Modern France
Neil Murphy

The French Disease in Renaissance Italy: Representation and Experience
John Henderson

The Many Lives of Täsfa Ṣeyon: An Ethiopian Intellectual in Early Modern Rome
Matteo Salvadore, James De Lorenzi, Deresse Ayenachew Woldetsadik

Who Owns Literature?: Early Modernity's Orphaned Texts
Jane Tylus

The Fabric of War: The Material Culture and Social Lives of Banners in Renaissance Europe
John Gagné and Timothy McCall

A full series listing is available at: www.cambridge.org/EREN

For EU product safety concerns, contact us at Calle de José Abascal, 56–1°,
28003 Madrid, Spain or eugpsr@cambridge.org.

www.ingramcontent.com/pod-product-compliance
Ingram Content Group UK Ltd.
Pitfield, Milton Keynes, MK11 3LW, UK
UKHW021145160825
461759UK00041B/300